Proven Track Record for Transforming Lives

"Lisa is both brilliant and beautiful. I've learned much from her wit and wisdom and you will too. Her proven track record for transforming lives speaks volumes and so does this fabulous book. Share it with your most valued friends and they will thank you."

—*Marcia Wieder, Founder/CEO of Dream University,*
author of 14 books and the spokesperson
for the Million Dreams Campaign

Added an Extra Zero to My Income

"Powerful stuff. I wish I'd had Lisa's incredible system when I first got started over 30 years ago. It would have cut years off my success journey and saved me a fortune in mistakes. Her brilliant system has added an extra zero to my income."

—*Robert Allen, investment advisor and New York Times*
best-selling author, writer of many best-selling books,
including Nothing Down, Multiple Streams of Income
and The One Minute Millionaire

Lisa Makes Business Easy

"Required reading for heart-centered entrepreneurs, speakers, authors, coaches and consultants. Sasevich makes the unsavory parts of business not only do-able, but easy."

—*JJ Virgin, fitness and nutrition expert, speaker,*
author of Six Weeks to Sleeveless and Sexy,
and media personality, co-star of TLC's "Freaky Eaters"
and Food Network's "Fat Chef"

Lisa Gets You Fired Up to Close More Deals

"Lisa Sasevich has a way of making you feel good about taking action. She gets you fired up to get more clients and close more deals and then shows you exactly how to do it."

—Sandra Yancey, founder and CEO of eWomenNetwork, ABC radio show host, author, movie producer, speaker and philanthropist

Make More Money Doing What You're Good At

"This incredible book shows you how to make more money more easily doing what you love and what you're good at. Lisa Sasevich is among the smartest and most insightful people I have ever met."

—Brian Tracy, author of
Earn What You're Really Worth

Worth Millions in Extra Income

"Lisa is the hottest ticket in the market if you want to significantly increase your sales and revenues from teleseminars, webinars or on the stage. She gets smack into the psychology of making the sales by presenting your products or services in a way that puts you in control and your prospects wanting to buy. If anyone buys Lisa's material, uses it and it doesn't work better than the traditional methods out there . . . they must be presenting to a dead prospect!

"I completed her three-day Speak-to-Sell Bootcamp and my last 4 speaking engagements have resulted in an average 45% closing ratio. This is literally worth millions in extra income to me."

—John Assaraf, an inspirational speaker best known from the film "The Secret", has built five multi-million dollar companies and is the author of Having It All *and co-author of the New York Times best seller* The Answer

Lisa is a 12 out of 10!

"I experienced Lisa Sasevich at the NSA National Conference and on the scale of 1 to 10, I was not able to give her a 10 for one important reason ... she was a 12!!!"

—Harvey Mackay, best-selling author of seven books, including The Mackay MBA of Selling in the Real World *and* Swim with the Sharks Without Being Eaten Alive

You Have to Get Your Hands on Lisa's Work!

"Lisa Sasevich is the undisputed expert on how to take your message to stages and teleseminars in an authentic way that gets big results. The first time I saw Lisa speak I watched in awe as over half the room rushed to the back tables to buy her packages. Once I learned a few of her tips, I saw an immediate increase in my sales and the quality of clients I attracted. If you're looking to create hunger and desire in your audience and you want them to invest in your programs on the spot, you have to get your hands on Lisa's work!"

—Ali Brown, CEO & Founder of Ali International and featured on TV's "Secret Millionaire"

People were BEGGING Me to Sell to Them

"I bought *The Invisible Close* in desperation when I was searching for a solution to why I wasn't bringing in the business with my presentations. I read it fast. At my next presentation, half-heartedly applying the techniques, I closed 10% of the room. Not bad considering I had been doing zero before. Then I went on to learn Lisa's Speak-to-Sell Formula. I gave my first structured talk and closed 1/3 of the room!

"As I was about to move into the offer one of the people in the audience interrupted me and said 'You told us you'd explain how we could take this deeper and I'm ready to do that, so what do I do?!' Another person yelled, 'I'm ready too!' People actually BEGGING me to sell to them? I was floored.

"At the end of my presentation, the president asked me if I'd come back soon. The person who booked me asked me to do a talk she'd heard me do earlier in the year and asked me to have a multi-week program to offer to the members!!!!!

"People were actually ASKING me to sell them MORE. This was certainly what I hoped for but I still can't believe it. I'm tearing up as I type this because I finally can see my business turning around because of what you've taught me.

"I can't thank you enough. Bless you."

—Winnie Anderson, Client Focused Marketing

Converted 73% of my Audience in 90 Minutes!

"The day I decided to stop being the best-kept secret in my town, I changed my life. Doors flew open and behind one of the doors was Lisa Sasevich! After my work with Lisa, I got on the stage and converted 73% of the audience in 90 minutes. No longer am I wondering how to present my million-dollar value to people — I know it, I own it and I'm clear and certain about it, thanks to Lisa's programs."

—*Dr. Sarah Farrant, DC, Founder and CEO of VitalMoms.com and the global selling and award-winning author of* The Vital Truth

I am Thrilled with the Sassy Mastermind Program

"I found Lisa through an email recommending her 6-Figure Teleseminar series. After taking that class and listening to her call about the Sassy Mastermind, I knew she was the mentor for me. Because I live in Europe, I have not been to any live events, yet the value, direction and support from Lisa and the Mastermind group has been incredible! I've been able to start a brand new business, using a completely new business model, and am implementing all the systems to build a sustainable, leveraged and profitable company. I am thrilled with the Sassy Mastermind program—it has given me the ability to learn and grow so much and start getting my message into the world to make a huge impact."

—*Karin Volo, Tough Transition Specialist and Dream Life Mentor*

Made $15,000 by Friday

"I purchased the Invisible Close about 6 weeks ago. This past Tuesday I gave a 45-minute talk and did the *2-step Decisive Action Scholarship* and made $15,000 by Friday. I'm now a believer! Thank you for walking this journey with me in service of humanity. Thank you Lisa for leading the way! You are my mentor from afar and I deeply appreciate all that you are providing to the world. Thank you. Thank you. Thank you."

—Dr. Venus Opal Reese,
founder and CEO of Defy Impossible, Inc.

This Lady Delivers . . . I Made $20,000 in Sales Within 2 Weeks

"Before working with Lisa, I felt really frustrated because I couldn't get my message out to the people who needed it. When I spoke, I would cringe when making my offers, and the same would happen when doing strategy sessions with potential clients. I started to question myself, doubt myself, and lose confidence that I knew what I was doing. I knew some people who had great results working with Lisa, so one day I bit the bullet, decided I'd had enough—signed up for one of her programs, and went to her Speak-to-Sell Bootcamp.

"This lady delivers. Really. She said we'd walk out with our signature talk, and I did. I also got super clear on how valuable I was and what I had to offer, and actually excited about "selling" for the first time in my life. I realized that when I sell, people transform. Not only did Lisa help me to realize that (she's a fabulous model of this), but helped me craft *how* to sell in a way that *invited* people instead of feeling pushy. The week after I came back from Lisa's bootcamp, I made $20,000 in sales within 2 weeks. The best part is that I made this helping people transform their lives. Totally awesome. I love this woman. Thank you Lisa for helping me get my blessing out in the world to 100% of the right people! You ROCK."

— *Anastasia Netri, Entrepreneurial Goddess Coaching*

The Most Recent Campaign Generated over $60,000 in Revenue

"What I appreciate most is your philosophy of 'build the plane while you're flying it.' I could have waited around until my program was "perfect" but instead got paid to develop a lucrative training (for me) and incredible transformation (for my clients). That first offer has become one of my bestseller signature programs.

"I have used your techniques in all my online launches since, including my most recent campaign, which generated over $60,000 in revenue. Thank you, Lisa!"

— *Elizabeth Purvis, The Marketing Goddess*

It's Like Being Given a License to Print Money

"I've had many quantum leaps in my business since I started working with Lisa but the one that has had the quickest and most dramatic impact is *Action Sales Secret's Strategy Sessions*. Lisa taught me as well as gave me a script for Strategy Sessions that I took and used word for word. I'm now closing clients into my high-ticket programs with one simple phone call. It's like being given a license to print money."

—*Bob Burnham of Expert Author Publishing, author of* 101 Reasons Why You Must Write a Book

Make the Decision to Learn from the BEST Teacher I've Ever Had

"Lisa's event was the best that I've ever experienced. First, I learned my life purpose and I wasn't even looking for it! Second, I easily created my Unique Branded System. And third, I walked away with "My Big Life Plan" which clearly lays out the next steps for my business. I've already completed a number of items on the implementation plan and my business is growing. Make the decision to learn from the BEST Teacher I've ever had. Lisa's teachings are second to none!"

—*Mujiba Salaam Parker, The Empowerment Queen*™

This Stuff Really Works

"I've only implemented a small number of your suggestions so far and as a result I'm already delivering a very profitable five-part marketing teleclass called 'How to Get More Clients.' I was blown away when I had people sign up for it from all over the world—Sweden, Germany, USA and Australia as well as a new client in Hong Kong. The results have totally exceeded my expectations. Thank you so much, this stuff really works—but then you know that!"

—Lisa Farr, Inspired Marketing,
marketing consultant and coach, U.K.

I Actually Look Forward to "Sales" Conversations Now!

"My message is truth; sales tactics and manipulation are the exact opposite of everything I stand for. With Lisa's help, I now know how to gently invite people to my offer in a way that is irresistible and never feels a bit like selling to me or the person I am serving. Within 30 days of working with Lisa, I'm finally getting paid what I'm worth, my coaching business is full and I actually look forward to 'sales' conversations now!"

—Alexis Martin Neely,
Family Wealth Planning Institute

Closed 50% of the Room, 100% of the Right People

"This is me doing a big shriek! I closed 50% of the room, have people still contacting the promoter to say they want to work with me, the promoter has booked a session with me and also is interested in my 12 month programme . . . I made £2,400 in sales—just from the attendees and I got 100% of the right people! This is all thanks to your training! I could cry I'm so happy!"

—Katharine Dever, Bettermorphosis, U.K.

I was Blown Away By All the Powerful Strategies Lisa Revealed

"A few weeks ago, I held a preview call to promote one of my programs and made a disappointing three sales. Then I attended Lisa's free preview call for her 6-Figure Teleseminar Secrets course and was blown away by all the powerful strategies she revealed. I immediately scheduled another preview call, implemented her techniques and made a whopping $14,000 in additional sales! And I promptly enrolled in her training. If I can get results like these from Lisa's free content, I can't wait to see what I can do with her program. Thank you, Lisa!"

—Ellen Britt, PA, Ed.D., Marketing Qi

The Results Were Mind Blowing!

"Just one idea I took from Lisa allowed me to easily and naturally add a more powerful sales message to my educational-style presentation. And the results were mind blowing. Shortly after I discovered Lisa's tips I made two 75-minute presentations to fairly small groups and generated over $85,000 in back-of-the- room sales! This was one heck of a return on my investment!"

— *Adam Urbanski, Marketing Mentors, Inc.*

The Most Critical, Business-Transforming Techniques I Have Ever Seen!

"As a marketing expert myself, I was hesitant (and a bit embarrassed) about hiring someone to help me with my sales. Could she really tell me something I hadn't told my clients thousands of times? The short answer is, 'Hell yes!' After nine successful years in business, helping others market their gifts, my eyes were opened to a whole new way of positioning myself and my product that I could never have seen without Lisa's help. The saying goes, 'You don't know what you don't know.' Well, have no fear, because Lisa knows. She is the expert's expert!"

— *Lisa Cherney, Conscious Marketing*

Lisa, There's Nothing Out There That Compares to What You're Doing

"Lisa, your work is fabulous and evil. You shouldn't be sharing all these secrets with people! It cost me well over 50K on my own to learn the techniques I learned from Lisa. I'm implementing the ones that I wasn't yet using in my workshops right now. I highly recommend your information to anyone who owns a business or is in any kind of sales capacity. Rest assured Lisa, there's nothing out there that compares to what you're doing."

— Stephan Stavrakis MCHt, Master Practitioner of NLP and Clinical Hypnotherapy, Motivational Speaker and founder of 3D Thinking

From 25% to 75% Sales Conversion after ONE Session with Lisa

"After working with Lisa, the very next week I started offering special session packages that she helped me design, and 75% of my clients enthusiastically paid for a package! Lisa also helped me to see that I was actually taking care of my clients better by encouraging and offering possible ways they could continue their work with me."

— Victoria Benoit, MC, LPC, Center for Extraordinary Outcomes

Your Mentorship Paid for Itself Immediately

"Before we met, my presentations consistently received rave reviews, appreciative comments, and helped people improve business practices. Yet, at the end of my presentations, my sales closure rate was dismal. Though I have a strong sales background and business degree, I couldn't figure out why people who acknowledged they needed my services still wouldn't buy.

"You quickly grasped my core business as we worked together on a presentation for me that is not salesy or pushy. I now share educational information with my audience, truly connect with them and convert sales! Your mentorship paid for itself immediately and I am adding new clients by effortlessly and authentically selling from the stage! This also allows me to help more businesses succeed!

"Thank you so much for opening the door to a lucrative new revenue stream for my business! Selling from the stage was a dream of mine, but you made it a reality!"

—*Lynn Redpath, Managing Partner,*
Pueblo Business Consulting

Sold $200,193.00 from the Stage in 70 Minutes

"Worked one day with Lisa and sold $200,193.00 from the stage in 70 minutes at the Glazer-Kennedy Info Summit!"

—*Ari Galper, Unlock the Game®*

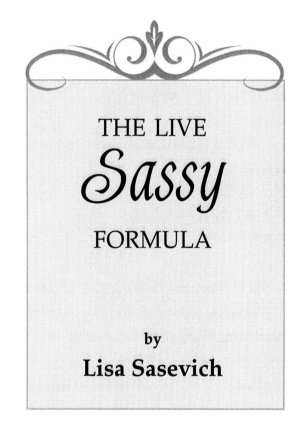

THE LIVE

Sassy

FORMULA

by

Lisa Sasevich

The Live Sassy Formula: Make Big Money and a Big
Difference Doing What You Love!

Published by Sassy Press, La Jolla, CA 92038

ISBN 10: 0-9852398-0-8
ISBN 13: 978-0-9852398-0-0

Sassy
PRESS

THE
LIVE *Sassy*
FORMULA
by
Lisa Sasevich

Sassy
SUCCESS STORIES

Step Two - Tune Up Your Sassy Mindset

Step Three - Make Sassy Money

Acknowledgements

What I love about this project is that it was completely sourced by inspiration. While the main chapter topics serve to outline the formula I discovered for living a Sassy, inspired, self-directed, action-oriented life, they would mean nothing without the thousands of Sassy messengers who prove over and over again that if you apply it, it works!

Thank you to my co-authors, the many Sassy entrepreneurs whose stories are shared with pride and vulnerability in the pages that follow, and beyond that, at www.MeetTheSassies.com, on the website we created so you'll always have a place to go to be inspired to live your Sassy dreams. As I have shared many times, I would truly implode without you.

This book is dedicated to my mother, Ina B. Garson, who passed when I was 20, and my father, Edwin H. Garson, who, after many years of inspiring audiences as a world-famous ventriloquist, took his final bow, ascended to the angels and inspired me to write the final pages of this book.

My mother had the courage to go out into the work world and keep her femininity while getting the job done. Thank you Mom, for making it okay to be an ecstatic woman.

Dad, thank you for keeping our Russian Jewish roots alive in your life so they could stay alive in mine. Not a day goes by that I don't live by your favorite mandate, "Keep your faith and your faith will keep you; faith in the Lord and faith in yourself." I'm sure I got my confidence, chutzpah and love of the stage from you!

I'm a product of the personal development era. My deepest gratitude goes to the people behind the organizations whose transformational work shaped who I am, including Landmark Education Corporation, PAX Programs Inc., More University Miracle of Love, and more life-altering books from the self-help aisle than I care to admit.

And now for my team. I count my blessings every day and wonder what I did so right that God blessed me with Peggy Murrah and Andrea Infelt, as well as Lisa Cherney, Michele PW, Andrea J. Lee, Nikkea Devida, Deborah Dubree, Ann Convery, Silvia Foster, Sharon Losnick, Stacey Canfield, Jimbo Marshall, Bob Burnham, Cynthia Lamb, Rosemary Sneeringer, Erin Tillotson and Angela Spisak. You are my true partners in empowering entrepreneurs across the globe.

Then there's my home team! A million thank yous

to my babies, Elijah and Sierra, who inspire me to be my best self every day; their daddy Michael, who, to this day, encourages me to "Never give up!"; my real-life super nanny Nadia who made it possible for me to focus at work when things get crazy busy; to my brother and sister-in-law, Barry and Juliet, who specialize in showing up for me and the kids at just the right times; and to all of my Sassy Mastermind Members and Alumni whom I think of and pray for so constantly that it feels like they live with me.

Last but not least are the incredible mentors and champions who came into my life at different times, some for a reason, some for a season—and many, I can already tell, for my lifetime. I am me because of you, Tim Kelley, Edwene Gaines, JJ Virgin, Joyce O'Brien, Stephen Stavrakis, Graham White, Ali Brown, Kevin Nations, T. Harv Eker, John Assaraf, Brian Tracy, Robert Allen, Suzanne Falter-Barns, Marcia Wieder, Kym and Sandra Yancey, Jeff Walker, Margret McBride, Steven Lees, Ciara Daykin, Kamala Devi, Juan Montenegro and all of the mastermind partners I've been blessed to share a brain with over the years.

To all of my current and future clients, fellow experts, messengers, mentors, supporters, affiliates, fans and friends, thank you for doing your work in the world. Thank you for being an agent of change. Thank you for Living Sassy so that others can too. Please ... keep taking inspired action! I love you.

> "Being an entrepreneur is one of the greatest opportunities for personal growth on the planet."
> —**Lisa Cherney**

What it Means to Live Sassy

Sassy. *adj.* 1. exhibiting boldness, possessing vigor and imparting spirit. 2. distinctively smart and stylish.

It is a bold thing to be out in the world doing what you were made to do. If it were easy, everyone would be doing it. But it doesn't have to be hard if you follow someone who has gone before you with a proven process.

This book is for the entrepreneur, or someone who strives to become one, so you can make your own schedule and structure your business to include all the things that you love to do and none of what you don't.

The Himalayas

This isn't for everybody. If you want to be an entrepreneur, it is a lot like climbing the Himalayas. You have the opportunity to experience the highest peaks of your life; the heightened moments you will likely remember on your deathbed. They are right up there with milestone events like your first kiss, getting married and having children.

But as we all know, peaks are not without valleys. Being an entrepreneur is one of the greatest opportunities for personal growth you can impose upon yourself. If you want to shine a light on your best "you," and you get excited about putting yourself into the most challenging situations mentally, spiritually, and sometimes even physically, then you will love this. If you really want the reliability of a 9 to 5 and the security of a steady paycheck, there is nothing wrong with that. This just may not be your path. The problem is that if you are meant to live in the Himalayas and you are staying in the flatlands, it can be very painful. So if that describes you, this book may be the answer to your prayers.

Which brings me to my own transition from the flatlands to the Himalayas and what all this has to do with Living Sassy . . .

How I Became Sassy

E ver since my early 20s I've been a student of personal development. My mom died when I was 20 and I remember thinking that at 48, she had a long life. Now in my early 40s, I have a different view of that—I have so much more to give. At the time, I was just finishing college and her death plus the transformational inner work I was doing took me right to my core. I knew at a deep level that this was not a dress rehearsal. We get one life, one shot—we need to go for it.

I was always concerned with making a bigger difference in the world, and how I could serve at the highest level. The energy of transformation fascinated me, and I've witnessed it many times in myself and in those I've had the privilege to serve. I love being a part of the process of helping people do what they are really meant to do in this world. And getting women to say "yes" to themselves is my passion because when women say "yes," they get to transform the lives of everyone around them: their partner, their children, their clients—and future generations.

Women have so much more influence and power than they realize. So when they really get to the core of who they are and what they are meant to do, they become unstoppable, and they want to take everyone on the bus with them.

Yes, it was my quest to serve others, and for some odd reason (maybe the influence from my Russian Jewish father who lived in Miami Beach, where I was born, until his dying day), I didn't mind making a buck while I was doing what I was passionate about: changing the world and being paid handsomely for it.

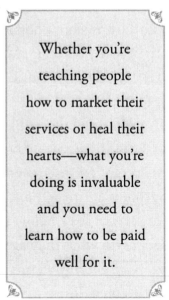

Whether you're teaching people how to market their services or heal their hearts—what you're doing is invaluable and you need to learn how to be paid well for it.

Very possibly, this came about because I encountered many broke healers, authors and experts during my years of personal development. Most of these healers were not aware of how profound their gift of transformation really was. And despite the huge difference they made, they couldn't afford to sustain themselves. They were masters reduced to beggars with their hands out, when people should have been lining up at their doors. That didn't make sense to me.

I knew that their vital energy was being sapped by

economic stress and uncertainty. It wasn't okay with me that the very people who had incredible blessings and expertise to share with the world were limited — in their own happiness, in their own lifestyle, and mostly, in their own ability to reach and serve more people. In truth, they should have been the most highly paid professionals in our society.

While witnessing this and continuing to work on my inner self, I took the traditional path. I went to college and graduated with a degree in marketing. I completed most of my Masters in International Business, and then I landed traditional jobs with big companies like Pfizer Pharmaceuticals and Hewlett Packard. I was on the sales team launching their new products and services into the world. In my 20s I was "corporate worker by day" and "personal development junkie" on nights and weekends. Eventually, by the time I approached my 30s, I didn't want to live a double life anymore. I began to search for a way to spend all of my hours making a difference doing what I loved and being well paid for it.

I was willing to get out there and let "the real me" shine.

In my late 20s, I also met a man just starting on his dream of becoming a heart surgeon. (Ladies, take my advice: catch him on the other side of becoming a doctor.) But that's how I was—a one-woman "build-a-man workshop." I would get them at the beginning and walk them through the whole process, launch someone amazing into the world, and then move on. But that's another book ...

I supported him for 14 years and I am proud to say we ended up hatching a talented cardio-thoracic transplant surgeon. The ironic thing is that I didn't stick around long enough to reap the rewards of the second part of his life.

I still love and adore him and I am honored to have walked that part of our path together. I would be remiss if I didn't share that so much of who I am today and what I've accomplished came as a result of our time together and his contributions to me. We are still close and have two beautiful children together. At the time of this writing, our children are 5 and 8, happy and flourishing, thank you God.

When I met Michael, he said, "I love you, you are the one, and I think you might want to check out this workshop." The workshop was

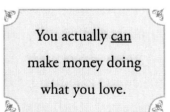

You actually <u>can</u> make money doing what you love.

for women, teaching them to understand and appreciate men. My first reaction was, "Why don't *you* take a workshop, buddy?"

But then I thought again and decided, "He loves me, I'm the one, there must be something he's seeing that I'm not aware of."

I took the workshop and it transformed my life.

So much so, that I have sent hundreds of women to this workshop over the years so they could enjoy the same transformation. I ended up becoming a teacher of this method and then became a leader within the organization. For six years I traveled around the country, learning to speak to women's hearts, teaching women to understand and appreciate men and learning how men and women operate differently. Through my marketing expertise (which was the first opportunity I had to spread my wings outside a corporate environment) I took a major hand in driving that business from $300,000 to over $1,000,000 in a couple of years—with no marketing budget.

Fueled by my desire for women to have the life-changing experience I had, I wanted them to say "yes" to themselves on the spot, so they could give themselves the gift of lasting transformation and have more peace in their lives, and I wanted to do it *without being salesy*. The old pressure sales techniques that pushed people to buy were just heavy-handed and so not *me*.

> There were industries of people wanting to get out there with their expertise who would have loved to have people say "yes" on the spot without having to become salesy to do it.

This was especially true in the setting I found myself

in. For six years I did everything from speaking at a podium with 100 women at the Hyatt, to presenting at a kitchen counter with four women in a Manhattan studio apartment—two attendees sitting on the bed, one at a desk chair, and one scrunched up in a squeaky chair by the door. I made countless speeches and honed my craft by being honest and straightforward so they could naturally make a decision to vote in favor of changing their lives for the better.

I wanted them to experience the transformation so badly that it became my mission to say the right thing, speak directly to their hearts, and provide my information in an authentic, non-threatening manner so they would make a decision on the spot to sign up for the weekend course.

As successful as I became at this, the truth was that if there were 100 women in the room and 30 registered for the weekend, I'd go back to my hotel room and privately I would cry about the other 70 women who had missed their chance.

What is it, I asked myself, that I could do differently so they could see that this could change their lives?

I started to pay attention to everything: what I said, how I set up the seminar room, the timing of different parts of my presentation, and I began to experience between 30% and 60% of the attendees saying "Yes!" to themselves on the spot.

Little did I know this would be the basis for what I now teach women worldwide around my brand, **The Invisible Close: How To Sell Without Being Salesy** and **Make Big Money Doing What You Love.**

What I also didn't know was that this would all come to a screeching halt in 2006 when the owner of the company decided it was time for us to part ways. I was devastated. I didn't know what to do. Although it was her company, it felt like my life's work was being torn from me.

> The Live *Sassy* Formula will not only teach you about taking imperfect, inspired action in your own life, it will show you how to inspire others to do the same.

Looking back, I can tell you it was a huge blessing and the beginning of an amazing path. As painful as it was at the time, I'm now grateful for that experience because I can see clearly how it all led here to you, on these pages, with me sharing real-life, first-hand experiences of exactly how to transition into your own life's work; how to discover your blessing, your expertise, that which you were uniquely designed to do.

The transformation forced me to go out and discover my million-dollar value. If you open your heart and mind to the lessons on these pages, you can make quantum leaps in your ability to make a difference in the world and make big money doing what you love.

Here's the beauty of what I'm about to teach you. All of the strategies and lessons I'll share with you in this book came from my training ground of teaching women how to understand men. What I know is that everything here works, whether you are a healer, an author, a messenger, an expert, whether you're teaching people how to market their services or heal their hearts.

Over the last four years, as I have been taking my own practices out to women and teaching them my model, it's been proven that this formula works beautifully whether you are teaching people something that helps them make more sales (like I do now) or you are teaching them to transform or heal their lives: relationships, health, finances, spirituality. *The Live Sassy Formula* is used by healers, spiritual leaders, direct marketing companies, service professionals (from doctors to lawyers to veterinarians, even animal communicators, *feng shui* specialists and every kind of belief change expert, coach and mentor around), as well as ritzy laser clinics that cater to celebrities, and solo entrepreneurs who are looking to keep a flexible schedule and maintain a minimal support team. As you'll see from the testimonials and success stories in this book, many of the world's top speakers and best-selling authors are now using the *Live Sassy Formula* to redesign their lives.

It's Time to Discover Your Million-Dollar Value

I decided to hire a coach. I believe in coaching because I know that those who have accomplished anything magnificent in the world solicited outside help in order to recognize their blind spots.

On our first phone session, my coach immediately asked me what I was passionate about, what I loved, and what really turned me on.

I started to share with him that what really turned me on was leading introductory workshops for women when 40%, 50%, 60% ran to the back of the room to sign up for our weekend workshop on the spot. I got excited because I knew their lives were never going to be the same because they made that decision and said "yes" to themselves.

And I told him it *really, really* turned me on when they would come to the first weekend that I would lead, and then take a further step — generally 70%— 86% of them would register for all of the other courses we had. Again, I explained it was because these workshops had made a difference for me in my relationships with the men in my life: with my father, my brother, men at work …

What turned me on, in a nutshell, was inspiring women, who tend by nature to put everyone else before them, to take immediate action to say "yes" to themselves.

There was silence on the other end of the phone.

And then he said, "Are you seriously confused about your million-dollar value? You had WHAT level of conversion?"

"30, 40, 60% of the women at the workshop …"

"AND 86% OF THE WEEKEND WORKSHOP?"

"Yes," I said.

"Do you have any idea that there's a whole industry of people out there looking to convert sales on the spot like that?"

I had no idea that there were industries of people wanting to get out there with their expertise who would have loved to have people say "yes" on the spot without having to become salesy to do it.

As I later researched this on my own, I discovered statistics showing that most people believed a great sales result was in the 5%–15% range.

Either there was a system to what I was doing or it was my stunning personality. I went on a quest to find out, and lo and behold …

It turned out there was a system to it.

Through that clarity and the process I will walk you through in this book, I was able to eventually identify

> It's my promise to you to give you everything I've got so you can know and feel in your heart what it takes to Live Sassy and share your gift with the world.

myself as the Queen of Sales Conversion. And it led me to systematize and package my expertise so that I could serve thousands of people all over the globe.

And *The Invisible Close* was born.

I took a big leap in my business when I started taking my own advice to make irresistible offers. I quickly earned about $130,000 in sales, and then, as I continued to apply the principles that you will be learning in this book, I skyrocketed to $2.2 million in sales in a 10-month period. It was shocking. It was a blessing. My then-husband was still in his last years of his cardio-thoracic fellowship in Tucson, Arizona. We had a one year old and a three year old. All of a sudden we had a new life and a new reach. We felt blessed and grateful that all of our hard work and focus on making a difference was finally paying off!

With the goal to do it again, I used the same formula the next year to take my business from $2.2 million to over $4 million in sales. As I write this, we are on track to do that again. We have served people to the tune of over $10 million in the last 36 months and it feels great!

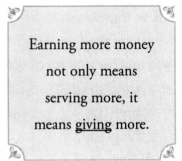

Earning more money not only means serving more, it means giving more.

I've been named as one of America's Top Women Mentoring Leaders by *WoW Magazine* and honored as a Foundation Champion for the eWomenNetwork for raising over a quarter of a million dollars for their foundation in 2011. It's gratifying to be able to use my reach and influence to do the things that I love. Earning more money not only means serving more, it means *giving* more. My business has given me the opportunity to contribute in so many ways beyond my blessing.

So now, I ask you: What's the training camp you're in right now? I had no idea while I was teaching women about men that I was developing my life's work that I now teach to the world. In these pages, you'll be able to find your million-dollar value and learn how to share your own passion.

My Sassy Promise To You

There's no question about it. Getting out there with your expertise is a courageous choice. My pledge to you is that I'll be as honest about what it takes to be Sassy as I am about the rich rewards of Living Sassy.

I'll deliver the secrets to finding your mission (I call it Getting on Your Dime), and I'll also share the mindset and the money part. If you're willing to open up to your own potential of how much good you can do in the world, how many lives you can touch, and how handsome the rewards can be, I'll show you just how far a book can take you so you'll have everything you need to get started making money with your "thing." And we have plenty of bonus resources throughout the book to help take you even further, should you wish to do so.

Starting on Your Sassy Path

So this, my friends, is where we start the journey. Through the pages that follow, I'll be sharing my "raps"— different concepts I've created along the way to get you out there doing your thing. I will show you how to get on your dime and how to clarify your mission. I will show different ways to go about discovering your million-dollar value and your blessing. I am going to teach you to articulate what you do and then dance into the spotlight and claim your space in a powerful and profitable way. *The Live Sassy Formula* will not only

> If your clients think you are the best thing since sliced bread, but there just aren't enough people who know about you, you'll receive simple ways to give prospective clients what they need to say "yes," and feel great about it.

teach you about taking imperfect, inspired action in your own life, it will show you how to inspire others to do the same.

If you have concerns about being salesy or being pushy, or if you feel blocked, you'll be shown how to overcome hurdles that may be holding you back. If your clients think you are the best thing since sliced bread, but there just aren't enough people who know about you, you'll receive simple ways to get out there making irresistible offers to your ideal clients so you give them what they need to say "yes," and feel great about it.

And while this is certainly a lot, the best part about the journey you are about to enter into is that it didn't happen to just me. This book was co-authored by over 27 amazing entrepreneurs sharing their Sassy Success Stories so you can see the principles I'm teaching applied in real life. While you may read what they have accomplished and tend to think they are extraordinary, which they are, the good news is they are also ordinary people like you and me who followed the formula that you are about to learn to accomplish amazing things in their lives even beyond what they thought was possible.

Although I am setting high expectations for the pages that follow, it doesn't stop there. Also included are many additional resources you will be able to use to live your Sassy Life beyond the pages of this book. If you'd like to get into action as you read, I invite you to join me at www.Sassy21DayChallenge.com to receive bonus training material and worksheets that accompany the teachings provided here.

Two of the things I am most proud of are that first, many of the masters that I have studied with are now my clients. Thirty-year veterans in the personal development industry that I studied with and high-profile speakers and expert authors have become *my* clients. You can see their names in the testimonials: John Assaraf, Robert Allen, Brian Tracy. They study my work and recommend me to their friends. It's a dream come true to be the pebble in the pond for these amazing masters.

I'm even prouder of all the underdogs I have helped—all the people that may never have gotten known or had a voice, but have one now. The difference they are making because they are using this formula makes my life worth living.

My Sassy Co-Authors and I have gotten together at www.MeetTheSassies.com to provide you with thousands of dollars of business and personal development resources to help you on your Sassy path, and give you tools of support should you choose to make this life-altering transition to Live Sassy. And if you've gotten this far, I know in my heart you're ready, and you will!

Step One

Clarify Your *Sassy* Mission

> "My blessing is to help experts who are making a difference get their message out."
>
> —Lisa Sasevich

Chapter One
Get on Your Dime

I've designed this book so you can apply the *Live Sassy Formula* and get out there and make big money doing what you love. The members of my Sales, Authenticity and Success Mastermind Program (my one-year training program that we refer to as the Sassy Mastermind) are able to go through my process together and support each other in various ways, by sharing resources and advice, by becoming affiliates, by joining forces for workshops and teleseminars and understanding what it takes to build a business as a heart-centered entrepreneur. You'll be meeting them and reading their stories in these pages, starting with this chapter. I'm so happy that they are sharing this book with me because you get to see how my system has worked to propel amazing individuals just like you.

The number one question I hear from experts and

from people who are in touch with their blessing and want to get it out into the world is, "How do I make money with my expertise? I want to make money while making a difference." We actually have a song written about this and you can download it on my Facebook page www.LisaSasevichFan.com. Just go there and press the "Like" button to download our Sassy song. And for those of you who are unclear about your "thing," we'll delve into that here as well.

I became very good at making big money for other people. I did it in the corporate arena for years with Pfizer and Hewlett-Packard, and in the personal development and transformation world. When my time ended with a company I thought I'd be working with forever (because I thought my "thing" was their "thing"), I had a big wake-up call. In truth, it *had* dawned on me many times, "I wonder what my 'thing' is?" but I didn't search for an answer because I wasn't forced to find out what it was. Sometimes if you don't take the little taps that the Universe gives you, you get the 2 x 4. As I'm sure you know, your biggest blessings can come wrapped in tough-to-swallow packages that don't appear to be blessings at all.

That's what propelled me to get out there. I was wondering, "What is my million-dollar value?" and I was feeling pretty distressed about being back to square one. How was I going to make a difference in my lifetime? But of course, I wasn't back at square one. Like so many people, I had a million-dollar value that I just couldn't see.

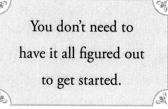

I was surprised by how excited my coach was when he heard that I closed such a high percentage of the room on the spot. I didn't realize that was something other people thought was hard to do. That's one of the first steps to identifying your thing. It's generally something that you do very easily, almost without a second thought. People will say, "Oh my goodness, how did you do that?" It comes naturally to you, but it's astonishing to other people. Unfortunately, that's why striving entrepreneurs, experts, service professionals and healers often discount what their services are worth, because they didn't have to struggle to obtain their gifts. But that in no way makes those gifts less valuable to someone who needs what they have to offer.

For example, I'm such a firm believer that making someone an irresistible offer is the best way to serve them that I do this very easily and authentically, whereas I came to find out that the rest of the world is terrified to sound salesy and be too pushy. They look at what I do, and they just can't believe that I can do this so naturally.

I realized then that my gift was supporting experts,

messengers, small business owners and anyone with something they're passionate about to be able to get out there as passionately as I do and ask for the order. I show them how to identify their thing, the mindset they need to make that offer, and the technique. That is what we are about to launch into. The beginning of *The Live Sassy Formula* is all about finding out what your "thing" is, and I call that "Getting on Your Dime." Because if you're not getting out there in the world with your unique gift, everyone loses—you lose the sale, the chance to bestow your blessing and the accomplishment of how great helping someone feels. Your potential client misses the opportunity to go to the next level personally and professionally. And the people they serve miss experiencing someone who is authentically themselves, and operating from their highest level.

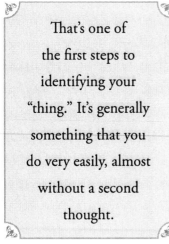

That's one of the first steps to identifying your "thing." It's generally something that you do very easily, almost without a second thought.

Moving Toward Your Dime

Few people are standing right on their dime. Life is a process of being able to see that fuzzy vision of our dime in the distance, and then moving closer and closer to our dime, with the lifetime goal of standing right on our dime. Even with the thousands of people I've been able to help, the millions of dollars I have been able to generate, I would venture to say I'm not totally on my dime. But the closer I move to it, the more opportunity comes my way. People are more easily able to identify that I am "the help" they need, and the heavens part for all the opportunities and abundance that I was put here to receive.

In the lifelong journey to get on your dime, sometimes you get on your dime, and then something happens and you see a bigger vision of yourself. You up-level in some way and suddenly you're back striving for your dime again. One great example is Oprah. For many years she was right on her dime with her TV show. After 25 years she must have seen a larger purpose for what she could accomplish, causing her to move into this next phase with her OWN Network. Her level of audience draw is completely commensurate with her being on her dime. Because her new network is still building, I would venture to say she's not completely on her dime yet.

Tony Robbins is a beautiful example of someone doing what they were made for. He's over 6 feet tall, with a booming voice, and hands that are three times the size of most people's. He has this huge presence and when he speaks, the tone of his voice draws you in and you're mesmerized. He was *made* to be on stage and to inspire people to unleash their power, and he *is* the picture of power. He is the walking embodiment of what he is speaking about. The more each of us is the walking embodiment of what we are sharing, the closer we are to our dime.

In my own path, I first saw that I accomplished so much simply by teaching entrepreneurs to inspire others to take action by making irresistible offers. As I worked coaching people one-on-one, and getting on stages in front of small groups, then with larger groups, it gave me a chance to get feedback about what people really wanted from me. I found out it wasn't just about the irresistible offer. But the irresistible offer represented a way the heart-centered entrepreneur could sell without being salesy. And that was what they wanted. They needed ways to sell, to attract clients and have them say "yes" on the spot to their products and services without having to be pushy. And I realized that I had a lot of ways to do that. And the more I wrote those down and found ways to distinguish them and express them, the more people came to me wanting more.

Discover Your Blessing

I'd like to share with you three ways to get on your dime, or at least to get moving toward it, so your life can open up in incredible ways. The first is to discover your blessing. Your blessing is that thing that you were meant to do. It's your work in the world. It is the transformation that you were uniquely created for and designed to provide. Chances are you have been doing your blessing in some form your entire life.

Tim Kelley, author of *True Purpose*, writes:

> Your blessing ... is when your essence moves into action. Think of it like this: You are a catalyst, a facilitator of some process. You do this process with those around you, probably unconsciously. Certain people need your process, and they are naturally drawn to you and you to them. This process is pervasive. You have done it in some form in every job you've ever held, and in every significant relationship you've ever had. You have been doing it since you were very young. When you are most successful and most fulfilled, you are doing your blessing ... Your blessing is the key to finding the right job or career. Purpose does not specify a career, but your blessing will help you understand which careers are the best choices for you. [1]

I discovered through Tim Kelley's work that my blessing is to help experts who are making a difference to get their message out. My mission is to help all people experience being known.

---

1   Tim Kelley, *True Purpose* (Berkley: Transcendent Solutions Press, 2009).

Tim and I met in a funny way. A student of mine told me Tim needed to work with me to expand his reach because his work was so good. Tim felt he should be touching a lot more lives. Within about 20 minutes on the phone with him, it was clear we needed each other.

You "Can't Not" Do Your Blessing

Finding my blessing in many ways has been the route to my success. It gave me the language to understand the difference that I've been making in people's lives my entire life. After finding the way to describe it so people could understand right away, I was able to speak about it, and the experts who needed me were able to find me. As my results suggest, they found me in great numbers. I want you to be able to know your blessing and be able to draw people to you so that you can help them and be richly paid for your services.

For example, when I started communicating in my marketing that I help experts who are making a difference get their message out, people started to flock to me, as if they were saying, "Hey, I'm an expert! I want to get my message out." They could just feel that I was the right person for them.

Your blessing is something you have been doing all your life. You can't help it. You've probably been meddling even when people didn't ask—you *can't not* do your blessing. While Tim teaches many ways to access your blessing in his book *True Purpose*, the one I found most powerful he calls Active Imagination. This is a process for finding your blessing that's really simple and yet very powerful. You ask questions and get answers. There are many ways of doing it. You can do it through meditation, through prayer or through writing.

The process that works for me (and, according to Tim's book, works for about 75% of people who try it), is the Active Imagination Technique. It is a two-way written dialogue with your Trusted Source, God, your Guide or Higher Self (whatever you are comfortable with), in which you ask questions and your own Trusted Source gives answers. It's a lot like the book *Conversations With God* where Neale Donald Walsh reveals his back and forth manuscript-like conversation with God. After Tim shared this process with me, I gave it a try. I had never tried anything like this before. I called my Trusted Source "God." This resembles a script between God and me.

Lisa: Hello, Lord? Are you available for a chat?

God: Yes, I've been waiting for you to show up and talk to me here.

Lisa: Wow! This is more than I expected.

God: Good. You should expect to get a lot more than you expected when you talk to me.

Just as Tim promised, I asked questions and started

getting answers, not just about general things, but specific things about strategy and how to deal with my love life, ideas about how to interact with my children and much more. Of course my skeptical mind wondered if it was just me writing back and forth to myself. In his book, Tim assures us, "That's a healthy human psyche resisting change." The more I did this process and took action on the guidance I was getting, the more I knew that these conversations were very real.

My Trusted Source would commonly use words that I would never use and have ideas that I would never have thought of. Many times this gave me the chills as the pen revealed the next action or insight. In many other instances, my Trusted Source was actually funny. Apparently, that's another sign that you are truly connecting. I've had the privilege to have Tim on my stage as a guest sharing this technique with many of my students over time, and I've seen firsthand how powerful it can be if you use the active imagination writing process to help you discover your blessing and get closer to your dime.

Clarify the Transformation You Uniquely Provide

Talking directly to your Trusted Source is just one way of moving closer to your dime. Tim and I call that the direct method, as in going direct to Source.

The second method, by comparison, can be called the indirect method. Instead of going directly to your Trusted Source, you go out and look at people you've impacted with your blessing to get clear on what it is. What you end up with is being able to completely clarify the unique transformation or outcome that you provide distinct from anyone else on the planet. There's no better mirror for that than talking to the people you've touched and helped to transform. In my business we call this "offer creation" work, meaning being able to say directly and succinctly what you offer to potential clients. You would be surprised that many people cannot say what their offer is or describe the outcome they provide with words that are clear and compelling.

This technique starts with identifying a person, preferably a client, who is your biggest success story. Whether they paid you or not, they took your advice, ran with it and had amazing results. The goal here is to find out specifically from them what exact results or transformation happened

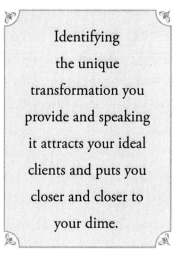

Identifying the unique transformation you provide and speaking it attracts your ideal clients and puts you closer and closer to your dime.

from their work with you, and then other results that came out of that result. What other transformations occurred in their lives? Listen to all the words that they say about the exact results they received as well as the additional outcomes that happened because of those results.

For example, if Jenny lost 20 pounds because she worked with you, you can note that down as a specific result, and then you would want to ask what other outcomes she received because she lost the weight. You may come to find that her marriage improved because she feels so much better about herself, she has so much more self-confidence that she got a recent promotion that she was passed over for before and that she has a lot more energy and vitality, making her a more active parent.

All these words can be used throughout your marketing channels, be it one-on-one, from the stage, on your website, in your book, to speak directly to the other people in the world who are meant to be blessed by you—i.e., your ideal clients. Fill up the page with these words.

And before you finish, ask one last question: "What would have been the cost to this person had they not engaged my services?" You may have to do some assuming here, but think about it. Would Jenny still be broke and struggling to pay her bills? Would her marriage be further on the rocks? Would she be feeling less and less connection with her beloved? Would her children be heading down the wrong path from feeling so unengaged because of her lazy, despondent energy? Again, you will draw from these words and use them to create hooky copy titles, headlines and marketing copy to be able to reach in and grab the heart and mind of your ideal clients.

The phrase "Make money with your thing," came directly from doing this exercise. My clients commonly also say they feel like they're "Tired of being the best-kept secret in their field" and that they are "Tired of reinventing the wheel." All of those words, which tend to draw my ideal clients and clearly attracted you, didn't come from some closed-door marketing think tank. They came from doing this exercise and communicating in the exact words that my clients use to describe their own transformation. Identifying the unique transformation you provide and speaking it attracts your ideal clients and puts you closer and closer to your dime and all the benefits that come with that.

Get Out There and Speak

The third way to get on your dime is to let your audience guide you there. Just as the sea washes a lumpy rock onto the sand and eventually hones it into a smooth, shiny, beautiful stone, the other way to get on your dime is to take the feedback of the masses to inch you over to where you need to be. This was actually the first way that I started moving toward my dime.

After leaving the company where I taught women to understand men for so many years, and wanting to figure out what I was going to do to make a difference in the world, I decided to just get out there with a vision of what I thought my "thing" could be. This is what I recommend for everyone. You don't need to know your dime to get started. I knew that all I could grasp with my fingers (and it really was just my fingertips, it was so faint) was that I had helped many companies grow and be very successful by helping them design, present and package irresistible offers. In the seminar and personal development business, I became masterful at taking someone who was interested and turning them into "invested" on the spot by packaging the irresistible offer in the right way.

> Was I surprised when over 60% of those women rushed up to the sales table to hand me money!

I figured I would get started with that, and I opened myself up to do one-on-one consulting and coaching for people who wanted to use that in their businesses. Very quickly it landed me a small speaking gig in Santa Monica, California for a women's business group. There were about 60 people in the

audience, and the woman who invited me had seen me
speak at the understanding men company. She knew I
could engage a room, so she gave me a shot.

When she asked me to come speak, she wanted me
to focus on what it was that I did to help grow that company from $300,000 to $1.3 million in a few short years
with no marketing budget. I sat down to think about
what I would talk about, and there it was—the irresistible offer. So I crafted a simple talk and taught some
principles about how to design and present offers.

The promoter who was booking me asked at the
end of our conversation, "Are you going to make an
irresistible offer?" The thought that went through my
mind was that I had nothing to sell. Many of you may
think that too, but here's what happened—she said, "I
think it would be really odd for you to talk about irresistible offers for an hour and not make one. Is there
anything you can create?"

I figured, "Sure. I could offer a bundle of three hours
of coaching with me, another bundle of nine hours of
coaching with me and maybe a starter pack that had
one hour with me, all at different price points."

Then she asked me if I had a book. I said, "Only in
my head."

That gave me the idea to do something I'd wanted
to do for many years—compile my expertise into a
book. Because I have a strong commitment to doing

what I say I'm going to do, coupled with not wanting to look bad in front of other people, this would force me to write my book. I presold this e-book I hadn't written yet, and I called it *Designing and Presenting Irresistible Offers*.

I got up there on the stage and made my offer. In July of 2006, I told the audience that in August, this e-book would launch for $197, "But you can pre-order it tonight for $47." Was I surprised when over 60% of those women rushed up to the sales table to hand me money for the book or for one of my coaching packages. I left that night with $1,800 and over 30 women who were expecting to have my first book in 30 days.

Nothing like using your ego plus keeping your word to drive you to create your first product. I wrote the book and I coached all those women who bought packages. What I discovered was it wasn't just the irresistible offer they were interested in. They wanted to know how they could make more sales and touch more lives without being pushy or salesy—and the irresistible offer was the vehicle for that.

That was my first moment of stepping closer to my dime. When I had that realization, I then had the thought, "Wow, I have a lot of ways entrepreneurs can sell without being salesy." I took a step toward my dime and wrote down some of those ways.

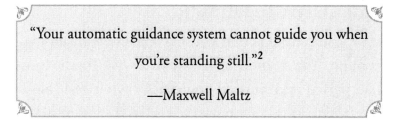

"Your automatic guidance system cannot guide you when you're standing still."[2]

—Maxwell Maltz

Through coaching people, getting out there and speaking and listening to client and audience feedback, I found what it was that people were coming to me to learn. Within a year, my brand, **The Invisible Close - How To Sell Without Being Salesy,** was born and it started right out of the chute as a big success, because I had moved so much closer to my dime. It all came from being willing to get out there and speak, even though I didn't know exactly what I was supposed to be doing.

If you are reading this book and you have been unclear or uncertain about your blessing, your dime, or the unique transformation that you provide, you can do one of two things. Number one, you can decide to stay confused. Sometimes that's just where people need to be. It is simply part of your path to be confused and it lasts for varying amounts of time for different people. If that's where you believe you are, honor that. You may not want to go forward with the rest of the pages until you come to a place where you get to number two.

---

2   Maxwell Maltz, *Psycho-Cybernetics* (Englewood Cliffs: Prentice-Hall, Inc, 1960).

Pick a Horse and Ride It

Number two is that you have been confused long enough. You're tired of it and you wish the heavens had parted and showed you exactly what your blessing is, but since they haven't, you're willing to pick a horse and ride it. You're willing to get out there like I did with some funky vision of what you're made for and start moving forward. I promise you if you do that, Source will step in and course correct you as you go. Think of a car with power steering that is parked. If it's not moving, it's impossible to turn the wheels left or right, but the minute that car starts moving, even just very slowly forward, all the power steering kicks in and it becomes very easy to steer. That car is you.

I want to borrow a quote here from Maxwell Maltz, "A step in the wrong direction is better than staying on the spot all your life. Once you are moving forward you can correct your course as you go. Your automatic guidance system cannot guide you when you're standing still."[3]

So are you ready? Are you ready to get on your dime? You can try out the Active Imagination Process and see what you get. You can look at the results of past clients and people you helped for free to get the words and the feedback, and clarify the transformation that you uniquely provide. Or you can just get out there with

---

3   *Psycho-Cybernetics.*

the faint vision of what you believe you were meant to do—speak and let your audience guide you.

My heart song, and one of my most favorite ways to teach entrepreneurs how to expand their reach in a big way and make a lot of money with their "thing" quickly is by speaking. In our Speak-to-Sell Bootcamp, we specifically work with entrepreneurs to craft talks that draw in just the right people that you want to work with. Members who have attended reported that with each talk they do, the feedback they get has been the best branding tool of anything they've ever done. Hours alone behind the computer struggling doesn't equal 60 minutes on the stage watching the faces of your audience: where they light up, what they flock to you for and what they actually buy.

I've given you three valuable tools, it's up to you to pick. What follows are three Sassy stories that will inspire you. They are a reminder we all have to start somewhere—but very quickly it is possible to crystallize what we offer and draw in the people who are meant to receive our blessing.

To help you get on your dime, join me at www.Sassy21DayChallenge.com and take my "Get on Your Dime Quiz." It will help you see what you were uniquely put on this planet for and get you started on your path to make big money doing what you love!

Three Feet From Gold

by
Karen Keeney

"Enough messing around – just pick one and let's go! If it's not right I'll let you know." In my active imagining process, my guidance gave me that message. I'd been following Lisa's work for a while, listening to her in my car while traveling for my corporate job. Over and over again, her teachings reinforced the concept of aligning with your mission.

I joined Sassy in June of 2011 and two months later I was laid off. I had to choose, and choose wisely and quickly. I decided I would pick my favorite thing of everything I've ever done in any job or business. I remember saying to a friend years ago if I could create a job where I could go to conventions every day, it would make my heart sing. She asked me why I didn't do that. I filed that away and ignored it for years.

When I found myself on Planet Sassy, as I waded through the Sassy training materials, every time Lisa talked about your blessing and your purpose I mentally plugged in "live events," and it slowly began to fit me. I started to wear it and feel it.

In my corporate job I was a regional sales manager and I brought our salespeople together through live events. In

my most recent job, I led sales meetings, opportunity meetings and retreats. Our company held an annual worldwide convention and I managed the speakers' needs and
expectations, making sure they got backstage on time, had
the correct flipcharts and anything else necessary.

I loved that. I loved being on both sides, having the
unique perspective of seeing through the eyes of the
presenter and the audience at the same time, knowing I was part of a connection taking place. I've been
involved in so many events, from being the host to
being backstage when there are 12,000 people in the
audience. I've always loved being in an audience too.
I'm an extroverted people person and I get my energy
from being around lots of people, but to be part of the
transformation that happens during an event is even
more powerful to me—that makes my heart sing.
When all of the pieces come together at the end of the
day, you create an amazing, successful event.

A few months into the program some more experienced Sassies said to me, "Just give it time. Around
month seven in your first Sassy year, we promise you,
everybody gets a major shift."

Month seven was January of 2012 when I went to
my second Sassy retreat. I remember setting the intention that if this is really my blessing, then I don't want
to go get a job. I said, "God, help me find two or three
Sassies who want to hire me to manage their events."

At that retreat 14 Sassies sought me out to talk to me! There was my confirmation and my reassurance.

I thought they wanted me to teach them how to do live events. They didn't. They want me to conduct events for them. As I'm getting more and more on my dime, my marketing is getting clearer, the way I'm talking about my business and what I do is getting clearer and my title is clearer: "Your Event Success Mentor." I was able to put together a very detailed proposal, which is something I've never done before. The clarity is even making those mundane pieces of running the business easier, and I'm attracting the right people to become part my team.

Recently I attended Lisa's Event Profit Secrets where I received even more confirmation—I'm going international! One woman wanted help with an event in Paris and an Australian lady told me no one where she lives is doing my kind of work. Now in my ninth Sassy month, I am overwhelmed with how much business is coming my way. It's more affirmation that this is what I'm meant to do.

Lisa's concept of not pursuing but being pursued is new to me. My sales training is "go get 'em, follow up"; the old-school way of selling. No one likes it, but it's what you do. If you're in sales you have a quota and you're only as good as your last month. But Lisa's way is to attract clients by tapping into their problems. Her problem/solution, problem/solution model is brilliant. As a Sassy, you get really clear on whom you want to work with and the problem they have that you will solve, and they find you. It's not chasing, it's connecting with your ideal client and being pursued. Your ideal clients know exactly who they are and whether they're supposed to work with you. I had to learn patience to let that happen, and it's so awesome when it works!

The Sassies Lisa attracts are wonderful. I walked in that room the first time I met them and I wasn't sure I belonged. These are brilliant, spiritual people who run successful companies, and here I am just getting started. Who am I to be in this room with all these people? Well, now they *are* my people. We support each other and connect in ways I never expected, and that's never happened in my life before.

Being an entrepreneur can be lonely. I have to admit I called a Sassy friend right before the retreat in January and told her I couldn't do it anymore and I had to get a job. She reassured me that everything was falling into place and convinced me to wait until after the retreat. She talked me out of hitting the "send" button for an e-mail blast of my resume, and then at the retreat the 14 people showed up three days later! Two months later, 20 more people approached me at Lisa's Event Profit Secrets.

So many people give up three feet from the gold, as Napoleon Hill says in *Think And Grow Rich*. When you have a group of Sassy friends who can hold you in a supportive space, you don't give up; you keep riding toward your dime with growing confidence.

Grab your free gift from Karen Keeney at <u>www.MeetTheSassies.com</u> today.

Diversifying the
Tenure Track

by

Kerry Ann Rockquemore

My Sassy experience shows that once you get on your dime, you can build your business around something even if it's ultra-ultra specific. I run an online center called The National Center for Faculty Development and Diversity. I help professors win tenure. Within that specialty, I help women professors in science and professors who are members of racial minority groups. That's a niche within a niche. My mission is to diversify our concept of professors, and who gets to stay and succeed in the university system.

I was a Professor of Sociology for about 12 years. Professors in the United States go through a six-year probationary period before they get tenure. In those six years of probation, you have to publish an enormous amount of research, teach, and do a variety of service tasks, yet in graduate school nobody prepares you for the job, you only learn to do research.

For me, the tenure track was torture. It was as if everyone had this secret knowledge about how to get tenure but I couldn't get anyone to tell me the secret. I didn't have any mentors. I had to figure out how to do everything by trial and error, making mistakes, being embarrassed, being so unnecessarily miserable that once I got tenure, I felt no one should have to reinvent the wheel and be this miserable again.

I wanted to create a space where people can really focus on their genius, instead of constantly figuring out how to navigate the politics at their institution. I started a program to help professors at my university and then I wrote a book and began speaking. It soon became clear to me that even though this program was great for the faculty at my institution, there were still a lot of people suffering and isolated, trying to make it through each day.

My book is called *The Black Academic's Guide To Winning Tenure—Without Losing Your Soul*. When I first started, I was only working with African-American academics and I learned very quickly that there are many commonalities across different racial groups that also affect women in science. Most of the time, they are the only woman in their department, going through experiences that are similar to minority professors.

How could they plug into a supportive community and get what they need to win tenure? I came up with 10 things people need to know that nobody tells you. I teach these 10 things and put together online communities to provide a space that doesn't exist on campus.

In two years, we've grown to 5000 members.

I left my very secure, tenure-track position that guaranteed a salary for the rest of my life to start my business full time because if people can learn these 10 things early on, academia will become much more diverse.

The road to tenure isn't just about how well you do your job, it's also about who you know, who does you favors, who tells you the secrets and who doesn't. The people I work with in my business spend most of their time with their students and they are great teachers, really investing in the university. They go for a couple of years and everyone is happy with them until their mid-tenure review. Then in their third year, they're told, "Your teaching is great, your service is great, but that's really not what counts. What counts is your research and you haven't published anything." Suddenly, they need to get their research and writing done, get funding to support their research, and publish, publish, publish in a very short time.

When I decided to walk away from my tenured position to start my business, it was excruciating. I've been a professor my whole life. I went to college, then I went to graduate school and then I became a professor—this was my whole identity. A certain status goes along with that. My work at the university was important and people were impressed by it. It was hard to walk away from guaranteed income for the rest of my life in this type of economy, and even harder to change my professional identity from professor to entrepreneur.

Yet, I felt like I was spending so much time on what I didn't want to do, while trying to carve out space for the things I loved. At a certain point I asked myself: why am I compartmentalizing the things I love in order to keep doing things I don't like? As scary as it was to think about leaving a tenured professorship, I didn't want to make the choice out of fear. So I spent a year doing both jobs, and then I had to choose.

When I finally left, I tried to go at it alone for about six months. I didn't know anything about running a business so I didn't know what I was doing. After a few months I decided to follow my own advice. I always told faculty, "If you don't know how to do something, go find someone who has done it extremely well, at a level that inspires you, and ask them how they did it." I found Lisa and it was very clear whatever she was doing I needed. The level of success she was experiencing, the lifestyle her business allowed (working at home, having flexibility and a low overhead) was exactly what I wanted.

I could have gone and gotten an MBA, but I didn't need a bunch of generalized knowledge. I needed a highly specialized online model, and I needed to learn how to implement it in my specific market. The Sassy Mastermind helped me do just that.

It was an enormous leap for me to become a Sassy.

Like many people who feel passionate about their work, it doesn't mean that you know how to run a business. That's a different skill set. Most academics think of marketing and sales as something evil, so the biggest challenge for me was to get comfortable with sales in order to be successful.

If I had kept doing what I was doing, I'd be able to help a handful of people at my institution. Now I have 5000 members at over 350 institutions and I am doing a significantly deeper level of work.

My first year in business, I earned $180,000, mostly in speaking fees. At the end of that year, I joined Sassy. I went from $180,000 to $475,000, which doesn't even remotely compare to a professor's salary. I can make more money, I can serve more people who desperately need it, I have greater reach and impact and I'm working less, all in a business that fits the way I want to live. Everybody wins.

Grab your free gift from Kerry Ann Rockquemore at www.MeetTheSassies.com today.

Becoming the Midlife Zest Mentor

by
Adele Michal

When I joined the Sassy Mastermind I was searching for the people I could serve best. As a psychotherapist for 20 years with a background in energy psychology, NLP, hypnosis and other modalities, I'd worked mostly with women and many sexual and emotional abuse survivors. I knew I would serve women, but that didn't narrow it down enough.

Lunching with a friend of mine at a Sassy Mastermind event, she confided that she felt so old, as if her life was over. She was 56. "You've got to be kidding," I said. "You've got the best part of your life ahead of you." My response was spontaneous and sincere. An hour later, she came to me with 11 pages of notes she'd taken from our conversation. "This is who you should serve—midlife women."

Once you start going through a midlife crisis, you think you're the only one experiencing the turmoil. There are relationship changes, children leaving the nest, death, divorce or recommitment to a marriage.

Parents are getting older, and you're getting older. Perimenopause and menopause cause huge physical and psychological adjustments.

I was almost at the end of my 50s when I explored this concept of helping midlife women, in fact, I was calling myself the "Midlife Midwife." I recognized I could serve them most effectively because I had gone through the process myself. Ironically, I believe it's even worse not to have a midlife crisis, to ignore the changes and to keep those feelings and desires all pent up. Midlife can be a huge opportunity, and there are many beneficial ways to capture that tremendous life force energy. The people who don't allow themselves to have a midlife crisis get old before their time and don't give themselves the opportunity to realize their true gifts and potential.

I've always enjoyed working with women who have their own businesses, mostly consultants and coaches, artists, and women with independent spirits, so women entrepreneurs fit really well as my ideal client.

As I started to get excited about my new venture, Create More Now, I saw I wasn't simply solving or "getting rid of" problems; I was maximizing strengths, hidden talents and sacred energy. I clarified the transformation I uniquely provide as: "I work with midlife women entrepreneurs to help them release old roles and outdated patterns so they can create their best chapter yet." I work with leaders who want to make a difference, and artists and seekers who pursue creative and spiritual fulfillment.

Margaret Mead talked about a phenomenon she called postmenopausal zest. I call it Midlife Zest, and I now call myself the Midlife Zest Mentor. As women have become more financially independent, we now have the opportunity to change the course of our lives and explore our own capacities after our children have grown and gone. There's an energy within us that demands expression before we run out of time. I think it's imperative that we harness this energy to give our gifts to the culture for generations to come.

When women think they are too old to give their gifts and do their work, everyone suffers. I have found that freeing women in midlife from the myths of aging is my mission and my purpose in midlife! I help them find their own purpose, which is critical to being happy and healthy into old age. What is remarkable about this time in history is that so many of us are expanding the definitions of midlife to create a radical shift in the expectations of what's possible. Youth is great and so is wisdom. Being vital and experienced is a rocking combination!

I've had other enormous benefits since joining the Sassy Mastermind program. I've been able to take what can seem so ephemeral (energy and subconscious belief work) and make it tangible, emphasizing concrete, real-life results. Now I can speak with authority about what I do.

I'd also been working for so many years in the dollars-per-hour system and I had to get used to Lisa's model. The whole mindset of appreciating your gifts, leveraging your work and charging higher-ticket fees made me value my own work. That allowed others to value themselves enough to invest in themselves, and step into the transformation of my work. What a huge paradigm shift! Since I've invested in myself at a high level in the Sassy Mastermind, I know from personal experience how valuable and life-altering that decision is. It also changes the way I view what's possible with my work.

When women, especially older women who have devoted many years to taking care of family and children, finally make an investment in themselves, they become so much more committed to their own transformation. Part of the paradigm shift is seeing that it's human nature to value what you pay for. I realize now that I am truly serving people when I ask them to invest in themselves because they can own their worth. I've had to learn that myself—lending a whole new meaning to getting on my dime. In my view, midlife is the ideal time for women to explore and express their true selves—when the time left to live is waning, but there's still plenty of oxygen to feed the fire of life transformation that is burning bright within them.

Grab your free gift from Adele Michal
at <u>www.MeetTheSassies.com</u> today.

> "The key to having people say 'yes' on the spot is being able to clearly articulate what you do."
>
> —**Lisa Sasevich**

Chapter Two
Say What You Do

To make a big difference and big money doing what you love, you have to be able to clearly express the unique transformation that you provide. The most important thing about identifying your unique gift and bringing it to the marketplace is being able to articulate it so that your ideal clients can immediately identify themselves and step forward, raising their hands saying, "Yes, I need help in that area."

We're not talking about any fancy marketing speech. You have to be able to say it using the exact same words that the client who needs you would use. The same words they would use with a girlfriend over coffee are the words you need to use to attract them. One of the biggest challenges that entrepreneurs have is being able to describe what they do and the unique transformation they provide.

> To make a big difference and big money doing what you love, you need to be able to clearly express the unique transformation that you provide.

In Chapter One, we talked about taking one of your successful clients and using the exact words they would use to describe the outcome they had from working with you. And if you are not working with clients yet, you can look back at someone in your life personally or professionally that you have helped. Because most likely there's an area where you are helping people over and over again, and it's probably an area where you do it very easily, but to other people it seems amazing. That's how you know you're on track with getting on your dime and it's that area where you want to begin to be able to articulate how you help people.

An example from my own business and my own blessing is it has always been very easy for me to encourage people to say "yes." It has always been very easy for me to make an offer to people. A lot of people look at it as sales and say, "Wow, it's so amazingly easy for her to sell." But in my mind, I'm actually offering people the opportunity to say "yes" to themselves so that they can have a better life. So what I do easily is something that astounds others and is really hard for them, and I've created a multimillion dollar business by paying attention to how I do what I do, and distinguishing the steps so that other people for whom it does *not* come easily can follow suit. There is an area of your life where it is exactly the same. You do something very easily that is difficult for others. In the next chapter we are going to talk about how to distinguish the system behind that thing that you do, but right now I want to focus on speaking clearly about it.

> Offer = Transformation + Service Delivery

We all have a unique offer. Your offer is made up of two parts:

There is the unique transformation that you provide, that outcome people can only get from working with you.

And there is the way you provide that unique transformation.

Whether you provide it through one-on-one mentorship or coaching, seminars, books, info products—we call that the service delivery. So there's the outcome or transformation that you provide, and then there's the way that you provide it, the service delivery. And those two together are your offer.

You need to be able to articulate your offer. In order to be successful at articulating your offer, it's important to focus 90% of your words, your energy, your attention and your description on the outcome or the transformation that the client would get from working with you, and only about 10% of your words or energy on how you are going to give it to them. It's important for them to know whether they have to fly to New York to see you, or if they'll be talking to you on the phone, or if they can listen to you on a CD, but it's only of 10% importance on whether they'll move forward with you or not. What propels people to move forward is that they want a certain outcome, that they want a certain *transformation* in their lives.

> Your clients are buying the destination, not the plane. Be sure to focus on the transformation that you provide, not how you provide it.

No one goes on a vacation because the plane they're taking has a good safety record, they may be able to get free peanuts and WiFi is available on their flight. They go because they imagine themselves relaxing on a chaise in the warm sun, peering out at a crystal clear turquoise sea with an umbrella drink in their hand.

A great example would be if you looked at this

book. You picked up this book because there's something it said that you wanted in your life, whether it was that you want to make big money and a big difference doing what you love, or the idea of Living Sassy appealed to you, or you were interested in the personal and business development resources because you want to develop yourself. Maybe you wanted a new model of doing business—you're a woman or a very smart man who feels trapped in the old way of doing business. All of these words that are on the front of this book refer to transformations that the book promises, and that's why you bought it.

Whether you purchased it online, you are holding it in your hand, or you are reading it on a Kindle, you didn't buy it because it's 328 pages and 65,730 words. You didn't buy it because it's a book. In fact, some of you may be listening to it on audio. It could be delivered as a movie. The point is that you bought the destination, not the plane. You wanted where this book will take you. The vehicle itself is not that important.

So when you're out there articulating what you do, it's important that you lead with the transformation, the outcome you provide, versus making the mistake most entrepreneurs make—and now that I've shared with you you're going to see it everywhere—they get out there to offer their products and services and talk about the service delivery, how many pages are in the book, how many CDs are in the program, how many hours in the seminar, and the truth is those things turn people off. We are all really busy, so confronting the amount of hours, pages, days and CDs it's going to take to learn your information will actually keep your prospective client from moving forward with you.

Describe the Transformation the Way Your Client Would

You want to make sure to speak in words your clients would use. It's always dangerous to sit behind your computer and make up fancy marketing phrases because people don't wake up and say "Oh, I need to fortify the nutrients in my diet and balance my electrolytes today." They say, "I feel horrible, I have to do something different," or "I need an energy boost," or "I really need a cleanse."

The language that you use must appeal to the clients you want to serve. For example, I had a client who wanted to use the word "doula" in her marketing. Many people don't know what a doula is, but her market is very holistic, her clients go to naturopaths, healers and spiritual practitioners, and they know that a doula is someone who helps you deliver a baby naturally. So in her own market she could use the word "doula," but if she were to try to take that concept out into the corporate world to attempt to enroll people into a new way of delivering a baby, she would need to find other words, for example, "Have your baby at home with the assistance of an expert," or "Give birth in a nonmedical way."

When I first started out, the most I could articulate was that I helped companies by crafting irresistible offers. So I got out there with that one piece and spoke. The clients who hired me said they loved the offer part BUT they loved it because it helped them sell without being salesy—and that's what they really wanted.

So I was able to incorporate *those* words when I started to market myself—using the same words my clients were using. (This too is a great example of selling without being salesly.) After that, so many more people were able to connect with my message because the transformation they craved was the freedom and comfort of knowing they had a way to make more money doing what they loved without having to become someone they didn't like to get the sale. They could be their authentic selves instead of someone slick, fake, pushy and salesy. Can't you just hear their collective sighs of relief?

A lot of my clients would come to me and actually say, "I love what I do, I just hate the sales part." And I've used those exact words for over four years. Right on my products it says, "It's for people who love what they do but hate the sales part."

Taking My Own Medicine

by

Kathy Marks

C oming from a successful corporate career in sales, I thought I had it all. Yet as my first live event with Lisa unfolded, I envisioned a much bigger picture for my career and my life. In 2008, I generated almost $5 million for the corporation I worked for and walked home with $300,000. If I created my own business I'd reap the entire rewards and have more freedom.

I knew I could do it; I was already doing it for someone else. Why didn't I just do it for myself? I sat there that day with tears in my eyes. It was so wonderful to affirm that I was going to take inspired action. The day I got home, I accessed LegalZoom, opened my business and started working on it 100% of the time. I'm on track to gross half a million dollars this year helping over 1000 clinicians worldwide.

In terms of saying what I do, I was known as "The consultant helping doctors drive revenue into their practices." I'd look around their offices to see if they were losing money in their billing procedures or coding properly for insurance reimbursement, and look for opportunities to deliver additional streams of revenue and better patient care.

Then I shifted my focus to teaching others how to consult, showing people like me how to do it better. But struggling physicians kept asking me to come back and help them. After being on the phone with several doctors one night, my husband said, "Why don't you take your own advice? You are telling them to do what they do best and leverage it to make money. You're not doing that. You're totally missing your dime."

He was absolutely right. That's when I started the Rx for Wealth Network, and the transformation I offer became: "Giving physicians the tools to achieve personal and financial success."

At the most basic level, I help doctors understand it's a huge disservice to their patients if they can't keep their doors open. Most doctors are in medicine to serve; it's a calling for them. But their current mindset doesn't have room for "I also need to eat." I tell them it's okay to have a good life, it's okay to make money. I don't want *my* doctors struggling. They're taking care of my most important assets, my health and the health of my children and husband. I want my doctors to have a good life. They deserve it. I actually have them repeat after me, "I expect and deserve to make good money doing what I love to do."

The first thing I ask is a loaded question because I know the answer. "What are you struggling with? Where is your pain?" The answer is usually, "I'm not making any money. I have to take out a loan. I'm going to lose my practice unless I do something." Not only is it about money but the medical oversight and regulations are overwhelming.

The doctors I consult consist of approximately 50% internal primary care and cardiovascular physicians; 30% holistic, naturopathic or homeopathic physicians, and 20% others, including chiropractors and dietitians.

As I examine their practices, sometimes the simplest things make a huge difference. Take for instance a naturopathic doctor who is not offering nutrition. Not only would this give their patients better service, it's a positive revenue stream. I'll also suggest exercise programs and supplements. I frame this as giving their patients the opportunity to at least embrace additional care that could help them and also keep their doors open.

I've walked into a doctor's office where there are three or four books on the shelf they have actually written. I always ask them how much their revenue has increased by selling their books. "I don't make money on selling books – I give them to my patients. My mom gives them to people who come into her beauty shop." It's really that bad. It's as if they've got all the gold right there and it needs to be put into a system so they can sell it to thousands of people at the same time.

Many times I'll be in a primary care internal medicine clinic working on diagnostics. The big revenue killer is sending everything out to a specialist, such as x-rays and ultrasounds. The big benefactor is the pathologists who are making so much money that their incomes in the last five years have gone through the roof, while primary care and internal medicine doctors are going broke. If a patient needs a nutritionist, they'll send them to one down the street instead of keeping one in-house.

The personal success side of what I say I do is a two-pronged approach. First of all, if you are making money and are financially successful, there is pride and honor that goes along with that. I work with Dr. Bob of Doctors On Purpose (whom, along with Lisa Cherney, you will meet later in this book), I think his program is great for my clients. He deals with the inner congruency, making sure clients are aligned, whatever that spiritual or personal alignment might be, and I'm the outer congruency.

I'm open to working with marketing specialists like Lisa Cherney and people in other areas to stretch beyond the box, considering options such as concierge medicine, a cash practice—whatever is going to help a particular practice the most.

I wouldn't have met these particular special people, Dr. Bob and Lisa Cherney, if it hadn't been for Lisa Sasevich and her Sassy Mastermind. When people call Sassies their tribe, they are so right. I can't imagine doing this without Lisa's teachings and the support of her team. From the smallest things to the largest, everything is handled. Talk about getting good feedback! We all get tons of support because we're all doing the same thing, always stretching our boundaries, and it is so comforting to know I'm not doing this all alone.

It is so fulfilling to open up new worlds for healthcare providers by following my own purpose.

Grab your free gift from Kathy Marks
at www.MeetTheSassies.com today.

Becoming The Wizard of Soul Purpose Branding

by
Sabine Messner

The name of my brand is Soul Purpose Branding®. Leadership authority Stephen Covey says "start with the end in mind," and I take clients on a journey to their highest purpose first and then translate it into their personal brand with my Soul Purpose Branding® Private Platinum Program. Through a powerful reinvention process we express their sacred calling in a personal brand strategy, then capture it though photography and finally bring it all together in a congruent brand so my clients can "say what they do" with words *and* images—totally knowing and owning their own spiritual essence.

As I look back on my life, art, image and identity, sacred ritual, solid business experience and joining the Sassy Mastermind all played a part in my divine calling.

I studied at one of Europe's best art universities, the Berlin University of the Arts. Admitting only 30 students once a year out of thousands of applicants, it took me two years to be accepted. I graduated summa cum laude in both Bachelors and Masters degrees in

Visual Communication, a unique curriculum at the intersection of art and design. Starting from the artistic perspective rather than the commercial graphics application, we were taught everything from the history of art, to typography, to communication theories to motion graphics. I learned what it takes to create a message through a wide variety of media.

When I was 26, I had a vision of my future. I was on a university field trip with my professor in New York City, sitting in Washington Square Park when I spontaneously tapped into the collective "American Dream." I could see thousands of souls arriving from the old country, landing on Ellis Island, and I felt the hopes of these ambitious, courageous people, shedding their pasts in the pursuit of a new future. As they reached for their highest goals, they erected skyscraper after skyscraper until the city itself became a living statement of human ambition in all of its glory and cruelty. I completely merged with this promise, power and beauty, when a bright shaft of light came down upon me and I heard a deep voice in my head saying very clearly, "Sabine, if you want to live your highest purpose, you must move to the United States." I was astonished. Then the voice said, "And you will find your highest soul mate." Then the light shaft disappeared.

Back in Berlin, my seven-year first-love relationship dissolved within weeks and I immersed myself in my studies. As I listened to music or looked at a great piece of art, I experienced the artists and their processes, becoming the art itself. My multi-dimensional abilities allowed me to connect with each artist's essence, the source of the art.

Three years later, at the dawning of the World Wide Web, I found myself in California being interviewed by the founders of the hip *Wired* magazine. They examined my portfolio and asked, "When can you start?" Being required to prove I wasn't taking a job away from any U.S. citizen in order to get a visa, I quickly crystallized and elucidated the uniqueness of my skills. I joined the magazine and together we then went on and pioneered the early Web.

Over the next two decades, I had gained a deep understanding of Native American shamanic practices. Oddly enough, my next calling was corporate America, never something I wanted to do, becoming the Marketing Vice President of a start-up company, and, eventually Chief Creative Officer for America's first identity theft resolution provider. There again was the link to personal identity, but from the shadow side—when you have your privacy compromised or your identity stolen. This led me to Arizona to find my soul mate, now my husband. Doing the career thing, I fell into a trap myself—selling out, yet learning much about leadership, setting up a business, and what constitutes integrity and personal power.

In my business, I take clients through a unique initiation process. Every client who wants to have a Soul Purpose Brand developed with me goes on a soul journey to two very sacred destinations. This is called the PowerReinvention® session.

The first destination is their innermost Soul Sanctuary. No matter how much a person has meditated or how spiritually developed they are, the power of having me hold space and witness them as they discover their Soul Sanctuary in a new way allows each person to go further than they could on their own. With new eyes they come to see their own soul as the foundation and wellspring for their business, brand and life's purpose. To Know Thyself is a core requirement to step into our purpose and understand our future.

Once they are completely re-connected to their soul, I guide them to the next dimension, known as the Upper World by the Native Americans, and which we know as Heaven. Here, clients meet with their soul mates, and receive all the messages they need to step fully into their highest potential. Finally, each client gets rewarded and honored for living their soul's purpose and fulfilling their destiny. It is truly reverse engineering with the ultimate goal in mind. This is how I am able to promise to position my client's businesses for life.

During the brand strategy phase, we translate the vision of a person's highest soul purpose into words.

That's when clients discover brands worthy of trade-marking: territory online, off-line, business name, expert title, tagline, signature program name, etc. It's all clearly articulated and ready to put to work.

Phase three is the signature brand photo shoot. Whether we choreograph the shoot on special location or go on a photographic discovery journey together, the goal is always the same: express the person's soul purpose, as close as possible to the original vision we experienced together during their PowerReinvention® session.

Phase four ensures the client has what I call beautiful Brand Art, including banners on websites, their ezine, Facebook and their social media channels for a cohesive personalized look. I bring typography into the mix and we view hundreds of different fonts to find the right energy so their brand really pops.

Because my business is so unusual, I could have undervalued and undersold myself had I not studied with Lisa. The business savvy and strategy I have learned has allowed me to position myself as a leading expert in the personal branding industry right out of the gate and charge accordingly. Joining the Sassy Mastermind has been essential because I needed an incubator and a supportive, empowering community. Meeting like-minded entrepreneurs helped me to understand my gifts, and, even more importantly, exactly how I could offer them to the world in a practical business environment.

What's more I *finally* get handsomely paid for living my purpose! In my first year in business as The Wizard of Soul Purpose Branding, I already live the lifestyle of my dreams. I have immediately gone global, working with fabulous women—and a few very smart men—from all over the world. I wake up every day knowing that I'm making a huge impact in the world by helping heart-centered entrepreneurs anchor and express their soul in their brand and business. Enabling my clients to stand out in a big way with their quintessential message creates a global ripple effect because they finally get to live their purpose, be the leader they have yearned to be and affect their own clients in a deeper way by working from their highest selves.

Grab your free gift from Sabine Messner at www.MeetTheSassies.com today.

Chapter Three
D.A.N.C.E.
into the Spotlight

Many of the entrepreneurs, small business owners, messengers and service providers that I work with, like you, are interested in expanding their reach. Some of them have been experts in their fields for 20, 30, even 35+ years, taking classes and getting initials after their names—doctors, lawyers, therapists and other specialists. All keep up with the latest information and are forerunners in their modalities, and yet their accumulation and sharing of knowledge has not resulted in a straight path to wealth.

I have a belief that if you share the wealth (and

---

4   Napoleon Hill, *Think and Grow Rich* (New York: Fawcett Books, 1960).

expertise and resources), you ought to receive wealth in return. By tapping into wealth, more wealth circulates in the world. It should work that way, but it often doesn't. Why? Why does going out and getting another credential often have no effect on your bottom line? If the road to prosperity is not just about collecting knowledge, what *is* it about?

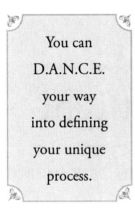

You can D.A.N.C.E. your way into defining your unique process.

Fortunately the answer is simple—in order to get your work out into the world in a big way, you need a formula, a blueprint, a roadmap, a system, a step-by-step process that clients can trust and follow. And the good news is you probably already have one—you're just not seeing it yet.

Discover Your Unique Branded System and Claim Your Space

When you distinguish the steps to the process or system you already use and organize that knowledge into a Unique Branded System that is *yours alone*, lots of things begin to happen. First, you're going to claim your space in the marketplace. The competition you had as a general service provider literally disappears when you have a unique system.

The second thing that happens is that with the systems

in place, you are able to serve more clients. You can suddenly teach the masses instead of being limited to only one-on-one service.

Third, you're serving them in a deeper way than you can even with one-on-one coaching or sessions. The system allows you to take them further.

Fourth, you make way more money. You can now leverage your efforts and serve more people deeper and faster.

By discovering their own Unique Branded System, many of my clients and Sassy Mastermind members have transformed their businesses. Those earning $125 or $250 an hour have been able to teach 20 people the same material in a group setting at $2000 to $5000 per person.

Not only that, but it's much more fun, it gives you more power and confidence, and it takes much less effort to sell what you do.

> You need a formula, a blueprint, a roadmap, a system, a step-by-step process. And the good news is you probably already have one.

Discover Your Unique Branded System and ...

Own Your Space

Serve More Clients in Less Time

Serve More Clients Better

Make WAY More Money

Sell Your Services More Powerfully and Effortlessly

My Invisible Close Magical Turning Point

I'll give you an insider's peek at how a process like this works, how a formula and a product are born. I was planning a joint venture series with another marketer. We had this great synergy together; our products complemented but did not compete with each other. His product concerned selling from the phone at a higher ticket, and mine was about converting sales on both the phone and the stage, having more of your prospects buy what you do. So we knew if we could show people how to do both, convert more sales at a higher ticket on the stage and on the phone, we'd have money squared.

We did the joint venture series together and people received extraordinary results, but when our conversations first began, as we focused on what we were going to teach, things did not go so smoothly. We both had testimonials from industry leaders, and there was no question that we both had a lot of value to bring to the table. But there was something missing …

> It became obvious that the reason The Invisible Close was invisible was because I didn't have a Unique Branded System in place.

As we started to look at what we were both contributing, for some reason everything kept looking like his "thing," not mine—it was as if I was his "special guest star." It was really bugging both of us because we knew it wasn't the truth. Yet every time we looked, all we could see was his blueprint, his Unique Branded System, but we couldn't find The Invisible Close.

So I had a phone conversation with my branding expert friend Stephan one night and he said, "You're having trouble because you don't have a system. He's got a blueprint, that's why it's so easy to see his steps."

That's when I realized that my *Invisible Close* book, my flagship product, was originally designed to be used as a reference book. Anyone could open the book to any chapter—for example, you could read the chapter on Live Testimonials, and go have results that day. You could open to the second chapter on Designing Your Irresistible Offers, go ahead and design your offer, talk to a client and have results the very same day.

It became obvious that the reason The Invisible Close was invisible was because I didn't have a Unique Branded System in place. And even though I've guided people in all sorts of professions to incredible results for years, we just couldn't "find" my method.

Then the light bulb turned on for me. And when that light bulb turns on for you, you can very quickly transform your whole business doing the same thing you've been doing, just by repackaging it.

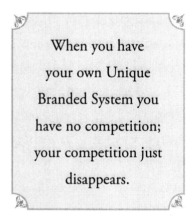

When you have your own Unique Branded System you have no competition; your competition just disappears.

And so I started to look and see the system that was already there within what I teach and I suddenly saw it everywhere! It was like shining a black light and having all the gold show up!

I even came up with a process for *finding* your Unique Branded System, and I decided to create a Unique Branded System for *this* system that I call D.A.N.C.E. So you can D.A.N.C.E. your way into defining your unique process.

What happens when you have your own unique process is that you have no competition; your competition just disappears.

Shall We D.A.N.C.E. ?

Discover your Process

> *What are the steps you use to get results with your clients?*

> *Separate your personality, credentials, etc. ... from your process.*

> *When you do 1:1 work, notice the parts you tend to repeat over and over to every client.*

Now it's your turn. I'm going to walk you through my D.A.N.C.E. system so you can start to see your Unique Branded System, the process you use to help your clients get the unique transformation that your work provides. I encourage you to put aside what you already know about how you do what you do and open your mind to seeing it in a new way.

The "D" in D.A.N.C.E. is for "Discover Your Process"

There are a lot of processes in your business that you think you need to do one-on-one. I invite you to expand your mind to the fact that this may be a limiting belief. Question the truth that you have to work one-on-one with your clients. I have clients who are body workers. They get their hands into the fascia under the skin to release aches and pains, and they're now teaching group programs!

In my own case, I always thought I had to do my VIP work directly with clients, so you could come to my office and we could craft your signature talk. (No one needs to reinvent a new talk every time they speak.) We'd get clarity on your offers and figure out how to reverse engineer your talk so that it led smoothly into your offer for a beautiful, seamless stage presentation.

I did this over and over with people one-on-one because it seemed like such a unique process. But after doing 15 full days with people over a period of six months, I took a look and found that 80% to 90% of the time I was saying the same thing over and over with each client.

As I analyzed what I did for these clients, I realized that my Speak-to-Sell process had 5 steps:

Developing Your Offer

Reverse Engineering the Body of the Talk

Seeding the Talk

Transitioning to the Offer

Maximizing the Opportunity

Those 5 steps comprised about 80% to 90% of what I did one-on-one. I taught the same things over and over regardless of their area of expertise.

Then there was about 10% to 20% on offer creation that really had to be done with me or someone trained to coach in that specific area. But when I looked more closely, I saw that even that had a process. Crafting the offer was a certain conversation I was able to mold into a process. Then I further leveraged my business by hiring and training coaches who can walk you through the offer creation process—the work we just did in Chapter Two.

It's just amazing how many more people you can serve when you open your mind to having systems.

Once I identified the 10% to 20% portion, the offer creation part, that I felt had to be done one-on-one, I was able to develop an intimate group program where we walked through that signature talk process over a seven week teleseries, and they received some one-on-one time from me on a private call.

It's just amazing how many more people you can serve when you open your mind to having systems.

The benefits may seem obvious, but let me spell them out for you:

> Number one: It takes me 90 minutes a week to lead the class.
>
> Number two: I'm making way more money.

But the amazing part that shocks even me is that the clients actually get a better result.

Why?

They're in an online forum with 20 other people who are all focusing on their Signature Talk. They can post the intro to their talk and ask for feedback. They can say, "Here's 5 hooky talk titles I'm considering, which one do you think is best?"

Because of this format, I'm able to post videos of successful talks so they can all learn from them. Not something I could have done when coaching one-on-one.

Plus I get to do Question and Answer calls and

live coaching. So anyone in the group has the benefit of questions posed to me by the others in the group. This is a great service because the question may not be anything they would have thought to ask about. They get the benefit of learning something they never would have discovered otherwise.

And these groups have formed incredible bonds, forging friendships, referrals and affiliate business partnerships, as well as supporting each other in a multitude of ways. Talk about a win-win!

Finding the System in What You Do

To discover your own process, you have to ask yourself: What are the steps I take to get results with my clients, to get to the transformation, the outcome, I provide?

This may take having awareness when you are sitting with a client, as the analyzer part of your brain starts to pay attention to the questions you ask.

Be sure to separate your personality and your credentials from the part of your process that anyone can replicate to get results. For example, if you're funny and charming on the stage, that's not going to translate to others speaking from the stage unless they are funny or charming.

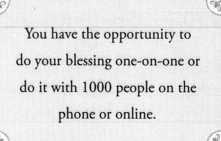

You have the opportunity to do your blessing one-on-one or do it with 1000 people on the phone or online.

While you may not be able to transfer all of your practice into a system that can be replicated, if you were doing all one-on-one/dollars-for-hours sessions and you could now complete 30% of your business with a group, it would still make a big difference in your profits.

But first you need to ask yourself: What is the process? (If there is one.) And if there isn't, if it's entirely based on "the unique you," then you don't have a Unique Branded System and you will have to sell by the hour. But I really encourage you to look closer. In most cases if it's your expertise *and* it's your blessing that you do every single time, you'll hear that parrot in your head saying the same thing over and over again—and that means you have the opportunity to do your blessing one-on-one or do it with 1000 people on the phone or online.

Aim for 3, 5 or 7 Steps

> *See if you can identify 3, 5 or 7 steps that you take to get results.*

The "A" in D.A.N.C.E. Stands for "Aim for 3 or 5 or 7 Steps"

There's something about odd numbers that seems to work: 5 Secrets, 3 Fundamental Ways, 7 Simple Steps ... I urge you to aim for an odd number. If you end up with 8 steps, you might see that two can be combined or if you have 4 Secrets, two of them could be separated to make an odd number.

As you work through your process, write down each segment and you'll be able to see what you can batch and what stands out as a solid, unique process on its own.

Notice

Notice which parts of your process you can teach to a group and which parts absolutely need to be done 1:1.

Question what you think needs to be done 1:1 to get results. Does it really? Or does it have a process too?

The "N" in D.A.N.C.E. Stands for "Notice"

Here is where we start to go even deeper into leveraging yourself and your process. Notice which part of your process you can teach to a group and which you have to teach one-on-one. And then really question whether the one-on-one piece needs to be one-on-one at all. Just like my Speak-to-Sell Bootcamp, you may find that you can leverage more of your work than you thought you could.

Are you going to be a service provider or a trainer? A service provider works one-on-one and trades hours for dollars. A trainer teaches you a skill that can be leveraged.

One of my mastermind clients does a form of body-work, and once he got to the "N" part, he noticed when he works with people that there's a whole aspect of his business he gives away for free on nutrition, and unique body movement, teaching patients to move and flow more easily. His teachings on movement are easily integrated into his clients' lives, keeping their bodies aligned well after they leave his office.

As this client and I worked together, we were able to break his practice down into four different things he does, and only one of these steps requires someone to actually be on his table. This allowed him to create different packages with and without the physical touch part.

The distinction here is: are you going to be a service provider or a trainer? A service provider works one-on-one and trades hours for dollars. A trainer teaches you a skill (how to acquire great posture or build a business like they did)—that can be leveraged.

For example, some clients of mine have a successful photography studio. They have contracts with the local schools for class pictures, they photograph weddings, events and shoot family pictures.

A few years ago, they were finding that a lot of moms were buying a $300 camera from Costco and starting their own photography business. So instead of fighting them, we decided they could become the business guru for the Debby Digitals with this tagline:

"How to Make 6 Figures with a $300 Camera from Costco Working From Home While Your Kids are at School." That turned them from service providers into trainers.

Create Hooky Labels

Play around with the steps and name each one with an action word or phrase. See if you can create a word, acronym or series of words that start with the same letter. Name the whole system, blueprint, process.

The "C" in D.A.N.C.E. Stands for "Create Hooky Labels"

I have to give you a little warning about this one. You have to go in order with my steps. Don't try to come up with an acronym first, such as D.A.N.C.E. Start with getting your process down. If you try to name it first, it can block you from seeing the process that's there.

What do I mean by a Hooky Titles?

Often a hooky, memorable title uses action words like D.A.N.C.E., or words like FAST, CLIMB, REACH. For example, another one of my systems is called ACTION Sales Secrets, which is a proven step-by-step formula for closing sales on the spot instead of dragging on for weeks or months with your prospects, wasting time, energy and resources. These Sales Secrets change the energy of the sales process so you're never in a position of pursuing clients or becoming salesy. The clients pursue you.

There will be some cases when you just can't find a hooky one-word title. That's okay. From my *6-Figure Teleseminar Secrets* there's a section entitled "The Five Ps to a Profitable Preview Call." So instead of an acro-

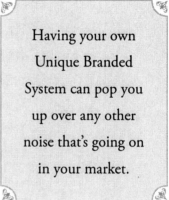

Having your own Unique Branded System can pop you up over any other noise that's going on in your market.

nym, I've substituted alliteration. No one can touch me in preview calls now. This illustrates how having your own Unique Branded System can pop you up over any other noise that's going on in your market.

I helped one of my former Sassy Diamond clients take her yearlong program and chunk it into a 10-week program, accelerating it and then asking $5,000 tuition. Instead of running these programs once a year, she could potentially run four programs per year, and run more than one at the same time.

Here's what she said about the process of finding a system: "When you're sitting in your own stuff, you can't see the brilliance of what and who you are unless you are willing to be visible, to show yourself. I was will-ing to put my 'all' down on the line. I was not connected to how I looked because I wanted that result—and out of that came my Unique Branded System." Finding and exposing your system can be a very personal process.

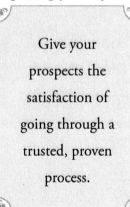

Give your prospects the satisfaction of going through a trusted, proven process.

This Sassy's marketing became so much more powerful when she created her Unique Branded System because she was able to delve more deeply into each step and talk about the specific outcome her clients would receive at each and every step. The same thing happened with my Speak-to-Sell Bootcamp. After doing it one-on-one, then creating those 5 Steps for the Signature Talk, I would talk about it from the stage, and people could get a clear picture of what we would be learning and the transformation they would have at each step— not just the one big fat result at the end. It gives people something specific and concrete, and yet comforting at the same time—the satisfaction that they're going to be going through a trusted, proven process.

And isn't that what you want? You want a step-by-step plan. This book has a plan. Teleclasses and workshops have plans. I doubt you'd feel comfortable if someone had a weekend workshop, and they said, "Don't worry, just trust that when you come here, at the end of the day, it's all going to work out." You would want to know about the system and the transformation you'd be receiving.

Enjoy the Rewards

Own your space.

Leverage your time (serve more clients in less time).

Serve more clients better.

Make WAY more money.

Sell your services more powerfully and effortlessly.

The "E" in D.A.N.C.E. is for "Enjoy the Rewards"

Enjoying the Rewards means owning your space, leveraging your time, serving more clients in a deeper way, making a lot more money and having a more powerful way to sell your services, because really, you've earned it!

Now you'll find it's much easier to talk about the transformation of each step of your program, "This is what my client received from this ..." and you'll be richly rewarded for having the courage to create a formula and name yourself the one-and-only expert practitioner of your unique branded formula, perhaps even crowning yourself king or queen.

When you get closer to your dime, you work from a place of strength and confidence and you're able to get the results you're looking for.

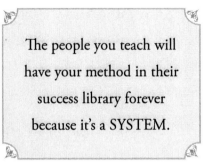

The people you teach will have your method in their success library forever because it's a SYSTEM.

Tip: Many of my own breakthrough formulas and ideas have come through the Active Imagination journaling process from Chapter One. You can definitely go to Trusted Source for this information.

Another key to this is to remember to use outcome-based words to describe each step—that's what makes clients throw their wallet at you—because they want the transformation, they want the destination, not the plane.

Really Good News!

If it feels like a lot of work to create your UBS, don't despair, I have really good news for you. You actually don't have to create anything because your UBS is already there. It's right on the tip of your nose, which is why you can't see it. I tell my students, "Put your finger right at the tip of your nose. Can you see your fingertip?" And they tell me they can't. And that's how your Unique Branded System is. It's so close. You're already engaged in it and it makes it nearly impossible to see without going through a process like this. But the truth is you've already been doing this, you've already been helping people this way, you've already been "meddling" in the lives of the people you love because you can't help but make a difference for people in this area. What's undistinguished is that there's a way that you do it over and over, whether it's by asking certain questions, directing people down certain paths or having people take certain steps. That's all we're trying to do here: Gain more consciousness and flesh out the system you already use so you can reach more people with your blessing.

Grab our D.A.N.C.E. Into the Spotlight Worksheet at **_www.Sassy21DayChallenge.com_** *and begin to discover the process you already use to help people transform their lives or businesses in the area of your expertise. This is also a*

 great way to get clarity on what your blessing is. And remember, the great news is, you don't have to create anything new. It's just about seeing what is already there!

Accounting for Lifestyle and the Unthinkable

by

Tammy Foley

I celebrated my 28th year in the bookkeeping business by attending Lisa's live event in 2010. I wanted to be around other women who were upbeat and successful. I was also launching an online accounting training program and I didn't feel comfortable with selling online. I'd already purchased Lisa's 6-Figure Teleseminar Secrets, so I was certain The Queen of Sales Conversion could help me with the sales part.

Sitting in the audience, I realized I was ahead of the game. I actually had a product and had set up an entire business while raising two children as a single mom. Then, one of Lisa's guest speakers, Tim Kelley, started speaking about Active Imagination. And here was this woman on the stage who had used that process to get in touch with her heart instead of her ego, and I wanted that kind of support, I wanted to follow my own heart. I was proud of my own 6-figure business, so successful I was able to send my kids to private school, yet I knew I was capable of so much more. I could soar with the support of Lisa and other entrepreneurs who understood what it is like to be working alone.

I'd invested in my children, clients and my employees, but never in myself. Now it was time—I took the leap and signed up for the Sassy Mastermind. I was literally shaking in my boots because I didn't have all the money, but I knew it was the right thing to do.

For my first year as a Sassy, Lisa came to the plate 100% ready to show me what I could do. Pretty quickly, I was able to free myself to reach the new heights I'd envisioned. I'd been wearing the hat of the business owner, the sales person, the bookkeeper and the manager, yet in my Day of Magic with Lisa, we mapped out a strategic plan around my needs and wants. From now on, I'd be doing only what I enjoyed or excelled at; the rest of my tasks went to my staff. I was free!

My Unique Branded System is called Pain to Profit: 6 Steps to Financial Clarity. The steps are:

1. Peace of Mind. I let clients know we have been there and that they are not alone.

2. Releasing the burdens and stress that are keeping them from being profitable.

3. Options, Strategy and Knowledge on how their businesses can be profitable.

4. Freedom from the unknown. Knowing what

they're up against financially, laws and rules from the government keeps my clients safe.

5. Implementation, Solutions and Follow-Through. To make dreams a reality.

6. Trust, Integrity and Success. These are entirely possible to achieve while running a profitable business.

Now that I was not limited to being a one-on-one service provider, my business, Bookkeeping Services, was helmed completely by my staff while I launched my new business and program, We Train U-2, featuring my Smart Entrepreneur Right Start Program.

When someone comes to me for help in setting up accounting, the first step in my Unique Branded System is answering "Where are they now?" then "What do they want?" We help identify their goals, dreams and aspirations. Step three is the strategy part, where we find the holes in their current system and offer ways to maximize profits and get their systems running as automatically as possible, to free them up to do what they enjoy.

My clients receive strategies and solutions of what they can do to accomplish their goals. I offer three Running A Smart Business packages. The first is a $297 step-by-step video course showing struggling entrepreneurs how to set up accounting systems and how to read a financial statement.

Plan two teaches the same system online with the support of being able to ask questions with a Financial Profit Detective CFO while learning. Plan three is our we-do-it-for-you option. We set up a custom book-keeping system and accountability program to keep the client on track to meet their financial goals.

Only six weeks after giving the reins to my book-keeping staff, there was a tragedy. My great niece was killed in a horrific accident. My nephew really needed me, so I dropped everything to take care of my family. I was there for 10 days, tending to six very young trau-matized children, and not once did I get called by my office. My staff was able to keep my business flowing smoothly by working as a team. After 28 years, what an eye-opener it was to see that my business could run completely on its own without my help!

Lisa was very supportive and nurturing through-out the whole ordeal. I would get texts from her with a huge amount of compassion, and the mastermind members offered their heartfelt help.

After months of mourning, I'm now getting out there again speaking. I didn't know how to offer bookkeeping from the stage. Lisa really helped me with that, and I've been on quite a few stages, even speaking in front of 400 travel agents. Lisa assisted me in crafting my offer and gave me different ways to increase my contact list. I take the audience from fear to confidence, bringing up pain points (being audited, missing tax write-offs, not being profitable, tax strategies) and pointing out that working with me is like having a partner in your back pocket who helps you navigate.

I'm now freed up to do what I enjoy, offering financial strategies to take clients to their next level and then advising them how to ease their tax burdens. I take them through all of their changes as they grow.

Since I've become a Sassy and freed myself of multiple hats, I've also been able to expand my business with offering online accounting to the many entrepreneurs starting an online business. Since so many people are struggling with this, it's been such huge financial advantage for me to work for entrepreneurs all over the country, and I will be teaching my model to other bookkeepers.

Having my Unique Branded System has definitely set me apart. I'm serving more people, making more money and have already made the leap from one-on-one service provider to trusted advisor and trainer.

In the first year as a Sassy, my business reached over $100,000 more in revenue. This year I anticipate earning even more. Today, I'm going through another process of freeing myself to reach a higher level using the exact UBS method Lisa and I outlined, only this time I'm even clearer on what I want.

I want to help other entrepreneurs, letting them

know they don't have to do it all alone. We are here to help! For me, being an entrepreneur is like being a turtle: you can pull your head in and just sit there, or you can stick your neck out and move forward. When you experience slow and steady turtle growth, you can make changes as you go, but when there are these big leaps like I've made, it can feel like you're starting over, and it's disheartening to feel you're struggling when you shouldn't be. With Lisa's inspiration I discovered that I didn't have to struggle at all—it was new growth. With these new problems of growth I was not alone. I want entrepreneurs to know they will have problems, but they're good problems, because they're stepping up to new levels of prosperity and achievement, doing what makes their hearts sing.

Grab your free gift from Tammy Foley
at www.MeetTheSassies.com today.

The Animal Whisperer with H.E.A.R.T.

by
Val Heart

I am an animal problem solver, animal communicator, trainer and healer, known as "The REAL Dr. Doolittle." Before becoming a Sassy, my clients were getting great results, but I didn't have enough money coming in to keep me in business. I had tried everything I knew to do and I was on the verge of bankruptcy. I knew I had all of my "ducks," they just weren't in a row.

The love of animals has always given me comfort and security in difficult moments throughout my life. However, at one point I was at a crossroads in my career, when out of the blue, a horse telepathically shared a traumatic memory with me. My mind and heart opened and I watched in astonishment as a huge knot on the mare's hip that was larger than my fist melted away so there was nothing left of it. Since then, I learned all I could about healing and ventured into a new arena as an animal whisperer.

Creating my own Unique Branded System turned everything around. It clarified my method of getting results, and completely set me apart from the competition. I realized my work went way beyond what most of my colleagues were doing because I'm a problem-solving specialist, not simply a communicator. Among other things, I evaluate and perform intuitive medical scanning on animals, apply several types of state-of-the-art holistic healing approaches that I am certified in, and invite dogs, cats and horses to become part of their own training process.

Now, with Lisa's formula, I have created The H.E.A.R.T. System.™ Every one of my clients goes through these 5 steps:

The first step is **"H," Hearing the owners and their animals.** I give animals a voice using the skill of animal communication. Once we understand what the animal is thinking and what they need, we know which approach will solve the problem. We invite their participation in solving it, as opposed to doing a lot of expensive guesswork. That's a critical first step. What makes me unique is that I don't stop there. I take it to the next level, asking: "How can we solve this together?" and "What needs to change?" And the life-altering question: "How can we create a fantastic relationship between owner and animal?"

The **"E" of the H.E.A.R.T. System is to Evaluate** how the animal's management, training and diet are being handled, and find out what is confusing and frustrating for both the owner and the animal. I ask the animal how they are feeling, if they are in pain, where the pain is, and when it started. Then we're ready to go into "A."

"A" comprises the Action steps needed to change management, diet or training so they work, taking a new approach if necessary, depending on what the animal has shared with us. This may include riding your horse in a different way when performing or competing. If a horse is resistant, messing up cues or their timing is off, we talk to them and work them through the process together. There's a way for the rider and the horse to get into a zone and merge their energies into one so their routine becomes a joy—effortless and easy.

Step "R" is clearing Resistance, which tends to come from risk, from fear, feeling anxious, tense or stuck. Whenever there is change, it can often create resistance.

Finally, "T" is Trust. By this point in my system, we have established trust, and when there is trust, we have the animal's goodwill. They are sharing their enormous heart with us. Horses will now do their very best to take care of us, to protect us and to synchronize and merge with us so that our rides become magical. This happens every time the client and their horse, dog or cat understand each other. Once trust is established, they all feel the difference.

Other communicators don't offer the action steps, training or support to get to this level of connection. Many cannot supply the medical piece, the training support or the healing capability, and don't follow up after they communicate. That's why I developed "The Art of Conversation with Animals," which isn't usually taught. However, I teach all my students how to do this because it is THE difference between being able to carry on a conversation to explore an issue, or being stuck or blocked in the communication. It is not enough just to say, "Here's a question, answer it please." Often animals don't want to answer the question, perhaps it's the wrong question, or the topic is not important to them, or they have been punished about this before so they are unwilling to get hurt again. Some simply say, "I'm not talking to you."

My work is all about change. It's about getting to the HEART of the matter. For example, stresses between a dog and his owner are mirrored and reflected by each of them, so by working with me, healing takes place for both. They find themselves in better balance, with more peace of mind and experiencing more joy in their connection. The experience takes their relationship to the next level.

In addition, I also teach people how to communicate the way I do it and how to apply the H.E.A.R.T. System™ to their own animals. I am developing extensive course work and hope to certify people to become professional H.E.A.R.T. practitioners. All of this is possible only because

I identified my Unique Branded System.

Now that I'm in my second Sassy year, I'm on target to double my income. One main reason I became a Sassy was to increase my list size, which was 2,500 contacts. After my first year I added 800. At last count I was up to 3,700 people. I have a podcast show, which originally generated 25,000 downloads and at present is well over 125,000. Now I am getting ready for my own groundbreaking telesummit as well as speaking on other people's telesummits. My big breakthrough this year will be speaking on stage.

Lisa's teachings have made a dramatic difference because I now enroll people into multi-session programs and customized consulting plans, created out of my Unique Branded System. With the program I launched last fall, 30% of my preview call listeners signed up for my course, a great return for an online launch.

The camaraderie among the Sassies has been heartwarming and wonderful. One of my Sassy sisters has even become a business partner. Joining Sassy has allowed me to leverage my gifts and transform the animal/human dynamic to a higher vibration of love, trust and undying affection. The grace and wonder I felt when my horse spontaneously healed fills me every time I witness miracles between my animal and human friends.

Grab your free gift from Val Heart
at www.MeetTheSassies.com today.

Calculate Your Fulfillment Factor

by
Julie Zolfo

fter my department was dismantled and I lost my dream coaching job in San Francisco, I spent 14 months pursuing lateral opportunities, with disappointing results. Feeling frustrated and defeated, I visited India for 3 ½ months to teach and to travel, determined to reclaim my own happiness along the way.

My newfound joy evaporated the moment I returned home, so sick I was forced to stay with my parents in Florida for over 2 months. I asked God, "What am I doing here?" and began examining my life. I concluded that when my choices made me happy, I was connected to who I was when I made them. When the outcome made me unhappy, those choices were not coming from my soul, but were based on trying to impress people, get approval or "get the job."

Prior to leaving for India, I had started my own private coaching practice. Yet I was struggling to find my unique coaching approach and whom I wanted to serve. Ironically, when I returned, I noticed I was attracting clients seeking to gain clarity on their passions. So I decided to learn more about passion, and I became certified in the Passion Test. This not only was a wonderful new process I could teach my clients, it helped me clarify my own passion for public speaking. At the end of the certification weekend, all students had to speak. I wondered what I would say to make the presentation more relevant around my experiences regarding passion.

I really wanted to impress Janet Attwood, creator of the Passion Test, so I started doing it "her way" but it didn't feel right. I realized this wasn't about impressing her; this was about honoring what she taught and how I would share that with the world. I can't be Janet, I need to be Julie!

I told the group, "Passion is very important and it's only one part of living a life. We just learned how to do the Passion Test but do you want to learn my formula for living a fulfilling and happy life?"

On the flipchart I wrote: P plus E times C to the third minus X. $[(P+E) \times C^3 - X]$. It just flew out of me. Everyone chuckled, wondering where I was going with this. I went on to say, "So often in life we make things so complicated. This formula may look complicated but let's break this down. I have identified six important principles. If we just follow these it would not only help us be passionate, we would be satisfied and happier."

This equation became my system. My Unique Branded System:

    P = Passion

    E = Emotional Energy

    C = Clarity

    C = Commitment

    C = Courage

    X = Expectations

I explained that **P** is for **P**assion. **E** is the **E**nergy expressed through our attitudes and emotions. Next I introduced the **3C's**. If we aren't **C**lear and not really **C**ommitted and don't have the **C**ourage to move forward, then Passion and Energy are not going to take us anywhere. Finally, we need to step back and subtract **X**, our E**X**pectations, learning how to accept the final outcome. And, that's when satisfaction and fulfillment finally happens. When it happens, it happens *for us* and not *to us*. What we think we want and what the universe gives us may be two different things and that's when unhappiness occurs. In other words, when we get attached to what we want, versus what we were given, that causes unhappiness.

Everyone was silent. Then there was this complete roar. Janet came up on stage and said, "Where have you been hiding? Well, you're not hiding anymore." I wasn't sure if that was a good or a bad thing, but she continued, "That's what you need to do as Passion

Test facilitators. There's only one Janet Attwood in the world and you need to take this work and keep the integrity of it, but share your own story in it."

Since joining Sassy, Lisa's UBS process has helped clarify my coaching formula further. My signature coaching process is called "The Fulfillment Factor Formula™: Six Steps to Making Decisive Choices that Ignite Passion, Inspire Action and Invite Happiness." To my clients, I am the Master Fulfillment Strategist. I empower them to bring out the very best of their inner self by making better choices through living with courage and confidence.

When I work with clients, we use these six steps as a framework to help them get clear about their passion and it makes our work together so easy. My commitment is to help people uncover their self-limiting inner dialogue: "I'm not smart enough," "I'm not good enough," "I'm not perfect enough." I help people get to the core of these messages. How often in life have we left a job, relocated or ended a relationship to think we're moving on to something better only to re-create the same situation we left? What's the common denominator? We are. If we can get in touch with who we are being, we can take responsibility in changing our perceptions, or shifting, which can significantly alter how we respond to life's experiences, events and situations.

One of my biggest shifts occurred when I watched Lisa at one of her events on a DVD and heard her talk about selling without being salesy. I will never forget that night, as I listened, taking notes with tears coming down my face. Lisa had a winning formula, a proven strategy for speaking to audiences in a way that was inviting, engaging and left people wanting to eagerly take the next step in their own transformation. I wanted to learn everything Lisa was teaching, so I attended one of her live events right away and felt I had found my tribe. For so long I had been the corporate person, told I couldn't bring spirituality into the workplace. Well, here was Lisa on stage talking about being guided divinely and trusting Source. It was because of Lisa's spirituality, combined with "Sassy" business expertise, that I committed, in the moment, to become a Sassy.

Today, I lecture at universities and work with innovative talent development managers and university students, teaching principles and techniques that help emerging adults, leaders and visionaries confidently explore "what's possible," by applying emotional intelligence, skills, desires, expertise and intuition, all part of the Fulfillment Factor Formula™.

Grab your free gift from Julie Zolfo at
<u>www.MeetTheSassies.com</u> today.

C.O.M.E.T. System

Taking Your Relationship Out of this World

by
Cheryl Blossom

How could couples counseling be done in groups and how could counselors be trained in a universal couples counseling method? I answered these questions during my first year in the Sassy Mastermind. Relationship counseling seemed so personal, individualized and complex. With Lisa's help, I began to look at what is universal in all of us, so partners could stop taking everything so personally and celebrate their differences. I came up with the C.O.M.E.T System: *Taking Your Relationship Out of This World*.

With Lisa's training on the Unique Branded System, I started to pay attention to what works in relationships. Commonly I'd see two people come to couples counseling who were fried and no longer having a good time. I used to wade in with "who did what," "who said what," but this approach can be a black hole from which you never emerge. Instead, I now get people lined up together to deal with the universal human traits that created their environment of dissatisfaction. That makes a huge difference.

It's absolutely magical for me to provide this road-map. It has made men much more comfortable. Before it was very difficult to get the man to counseling unless the woman threatened to leave him. He didn't want to talk because every time he and his partner talked they would fight. Men appreciate the C.O.M.E.T. System because it's task-oriented and they can take action to solve problems.

Now with the C.O.M.E.T. System, I get couples started off looking at the universal mainstays of a rela-tionship. The number one thing I found that is univer-sal is that everyone has values.

C is for Clarify Your Values. What guarantees a recurring and never-ending fight? When we do not recognize or honor that our partner may have different values. If an individual isn't clear what their own val-ues are, they won't notice let alone respect their part-ner's values. It's important for each person to know what their own values are.

If somebody is security-minded, a saver, then being thrifty is part of their value system. If they marry someone who is spontaneous, loves to be adventur-ous and is free spending, at some point there will be a breakdown as a result of these very different values.

The saver will think the other person is wrong. Once you start to identify your own personal values, you either appreciate how your partner is wired, or discover that how they are wired isn't going to work for you and you cannot continue to have a relationship with them.

A security-minded planner will feel threatened by a spontaneous person and become controlling, wanting their partner to become more like they are. Often we are attracted to our opposites because that trait is missing in ourselves.

Doing this program isn't about the right way to be. It's really about getting clear. Core values are the filters by which we live our lives. If a couple is constantly fighting about core values, it's going to be too difficult to bridge the gap.

O is for Offer Up Fun. By the time people come to see me they are no longer having any fun; by creating and having fun, their relationship is transformed. People may have an expectation that their partner is supposed to make them happy, and they are not clear what it is that they find fun anymore.

I have couples individually create a menu of fun things they like to do. Then they order off each other's menu.

When you order off your partner's menu, your job is to deliver as much fun as possible around whatever they want. When people start to generate fun it's different than hoping that it will be fun or that their partner will create the fun. When people are responsible for generating the fun, they find a way of being together that is lighthearted and pleasurable.

M is for Mission Statements. We are pretty clear about writing mission statements for businesses. For couples, many times a mission is to have children together, after that, the aim of the relationship can get lost. What is your vision for the future of your relationship? Where is it going? What are the ground rules? The old quote, "Vision makes problems obsolete" is really true for relationships. If you have a vision about what your relationship will contribute to your life or to your partner's life and that is spelled out in a mission statement, then there's not a lot of confusion about expectations. There is no longer a mystery about what is not working.

What is fascinating about this step is that people start to generate satisfaction in their relationship once they get clear about why they are with this person. Some of the complaints and bickering go away because they've stopped wondering if they want to be with their partner.

The difference this is making both for couples I work with and for therapists I train is amazing.

E is for Efficient and Effective Communication Tools. Simple tools foster respectful communication. For example, when one partner is upset, I tell them not to start their conversation with "You." "You did XYZ ..."

Start with "I." "I think ..."or "I feel ..." With "I," the person invites their partner into their universe, and their partner doesn't have to defend themselves.

Another tool is noticing if their partner is full. If they have way too much on their plate and cannot take in any more, a blowup is imminent. When someone comes home and they've had struggles all day at work, they are full. Give them an opportunity to empty. Get into their universe, ask them questions about their day. This will help them empty out; then you will have some space to communicate into.

Another key piece is timing. Women are notorious for lobbing a hand grenade of communication at their partner as he is walking out the door, because they are afraid of confrontation. Ask your partner if it is a good time to talk. If it isn't, set up a time that will work for both of you. Create the time and space to be heard.

T is for Transcending the Mundane. Couples can slide into expecting that it is the other person's job to turn them on. However , if someone isn't passionate about themselves, passionate about their life, or know what turns themselves on, it is going to be next to impossible for their partner to turn them on. T is for turn yourself on; transcend the ordinary. What are some ways to turn yourself on to yourself, to your partner, to life?

Some suggestions are setting up your room as if a

dignitary or a rock star is coming for a visit (surprise your partner, they are the special guest). Do a "word of the week," and generate that whole week around that word. So if you pick "silly," the whole week is spent exploring what is silly. Accentuating the positive generates more positive outcomes.

The beauty of the C.O.M.E.T. System is that the counselor and the two individuals avoid getting sucked into the games people can play, couples become clear that they are 100% responsible for their relationship and they learn useful tools to shift their relationship in a positive direction.

Since joining Sassy, I received so much support for coming up with and building my C.O.M.E.T. System, and now I'm creating my school and taking it out on the Internet. None of this would be possible if I hadn't followed Lisa's advice and created a system around my work. It's like magic. The system is what makes it possible to serve hundreds or thousands of people around the world at the same time. Before that I was tied to only being able to serve people one-by-one. Because of this, my profits are steadily increasing. My second Sassy year is about getting more radio and speaking engagements, and leveraging my system into the international community.

I see Lisa as a visionary making an enormous difference for thousands of people worldwide. Her business model of getting paid for what you provide is the ticket in, but the best part is Lisa really offers an opportunity for entrepreneurs to become profoundly fulfilled. For me, this means touching the planet with my C.O.M.E.T. System to transform countless relationships by honoring values, respect, shared vision, communication ... and something that gets lost along the way—fun!

Grab your free gift from Cheryl Blossom
at www.MeetTheSassies.com today.

Step Two
Tune Up Your *Sassy* Mindset

> "Rather than waiting for someone to crown you, you need to step up to the throne and crown yourself."
>
> —Lisa Sasevich

Chapter Four
Assume the Throne

Assuming the throne is about owning your gifts by stepping up and crowning yourself the queen or king, it's not about not being too shy or too small to stand up and declare yourself the expert in your field. It's not about ego; it's about shining your light, sharing your talents and claiming your space.

I always knew I had an awesome gift—just as you do. I knew there was something special about the way I helped people and businesses recognize opportunities, how I could inspire people to say "yes" to themselves so they could move forward in their lives. When I worked in the corporate world, I excelled at certain things. While working for Pfizer as a brand-new pharmaceutical rep, I won all the top sales awards, even though many employees had been there years longer than I had. I also won contests involving catchy titles—I have a knack for names that draw people in and stick in their minds. When they held a contest to name the company newsletter, I was the one who came up with the title.

So my special gifts were marketing, sales and inspiring people, and I just figured if I stayed out there doing my thing long enough, someone would discover me.

I waited and waited through my 20s, my 30s, and when I got to my 40s nobody had knocked on my door saying, "Hey, we heard that you're really great at attracting people and making people comfortable quickly." Nobody came and granted me my own TV show or told me, "We want you to star in our infomercial" or "Would you be the keynote speaker? Because we heard about all the great things you did." I realized at some point that I was going to have to just assume the throne.

> Being able to name the area where you claim your space as king or queen is an essential part of being on the throne.

For me the big day came when I flashed on my expert title, "The Queen of Sales Conversion." I discovered there was an area of my life where I could take all the different things that I do and give them an umbrella title. All these qualities fell under sales conversion: being able to inspire people to say "yes" (which is converting a sale), helping them to convert sales through irresistible offers on stages, via teleseminars, and one-on-one. *The Invisible Close* is about sales conversion, my program called 6-Figure Teleseminar Secrets deals with converting sales on the phone, and my Speak-to-Sell Bootcamp teaches clients how to convert sales from the stage. All these different interesting areas that looked so unrelated actually fell under this umbrella of transformation.

Being able to name the area where you claim your space as king or queen is an essential part of being on the throne. And by the way, I do not recommend that everybody go out and be the queen of X. It just so happened in my case it worked out nicely for me, but it may not be right for you. Words people often use are expert, guru, mentor and specialist.

One of my clients calls herself the Accelerated Results Specialist. She assumes the throne by accelerating people's results beyond what they ever thought possible. Another is the Juicy Marketing Expert. In marketing, she holds the space for helping people to get juicy words to describe what they do. Another client is called the Recurring Revenue Expert. She has created a space for herself and assumed the throne by helping people who want to create steady, repeated revenue.

Your title should explain the transformation in it.

The first workshop I ever invested in was called

the Online Success Blueprint workshop. The transformation is in the name. People think, "I want Online Success. She's going to give me a blueprint. Great!" I offer the Speak-to-Sell Bootcamp where we teach my Speak-to-Sell Formula. That's what you want when you get on stage. Not a script, but a formula. Another friend of mine is the King of Product Launches. He's the person to go to for the Product Launch Formula. You want to launch a product, use his formula. And I have 6-Figure Teleseminar Secrets where we walk you through the formula for 6-figure teleseminars to learn how to publicize the event, get large numbers of people signed up, and how to keep getting clients to sign up for the programs or product you're launching even after the teleseminar date.

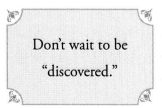

Don't wait to be "discovered."

We've all heard those life-changing stories about people who were "discovered." A woman was just walking around at a swap meet and someone recognized how beautiful she was and the next thing you know, she's a supermodel. You often hear about someone being transported to fame, such as becoming an Angel in the "Victoria's Secret Fashion Show." They saw this woman at an outdoor market in Italy, couldn't believe her beauty, got her in for a photo shoot and now she's the top model for Victoria's Secret ...

Well, the reason these stories stand out is because they are few and far between. So rather than waiting for someone to crown you, you need to step up to the throne and crown yourself.

In the last chapter, I related that a lot of people are going to college and beyond, getting diplomas and certifications, thinking if they just get enough letters after their names someone will crown them—and it still doesn't happen. College courses and certifications are great for expanding your knowledge base and your credibility, but if you think this will lead to becoming an industry leader, in most cases it does not.

> If you could crown yourself king or queen of some land, what would it be?

So what are your credentials? What have you been doing for five years? 10 years? 20 years? (Some expertise perhaps you've never been paid for.) If you could crown yourself king or queen of some land, what would it be? If someone were to discover you and crown you, what would it be for?

Giving Yourself an Expert Title

1. What are you the queen or king or expert of?

2. How would you describe the throne that you sit on, the space that you occupy?

The title should explain the transformation in it. The title should help people understand what you do. One of the Sassies featured in this book used the title "Midlife Midwife," because she was helping people with the second half of their lives. Although this is a great title and it worked in this case, one tip I have is never substitute cute for effective. Sometimes we get stuck on names that rhyme or are snappy in some way, but they don't really communicate what we do in the title. Make sure that your expert title describes the transformation that you provide.

When you first assume the throne in your space, it's a little uncomfortable. You wonder if someone's going to come and ask for your credentials. How do I know I'm the Queen of Sales Conversion? Where's my certificate? The truth is I don't have one, but I have over 20 years of inspiring people to say "yes" on the spot—that's my credential. It's a self-given credential. Remember that it's your land—you created it—and it's your throne. You wouldn't have crowned yourself if you didn't have sufficient mojo in that area. The point of assuming the throne is to stop waiting for someone else to discover you. Go ahead and take your seat at the head of the table.

The ER Doctor for the Heart and Soul

by
Dr. Bob Uslander

I've practiced emergency medicine for the past 20 years. About 10 years into my career, medicine started to shift and I recognized that more and more people in healthcare were not happy. I was mostly content, but having a hard time envisioning doing the same job for the next 20 or 30 years—and things were not likely to get a lot better.

I liked being an ER doctor because it was meaningful to society, and it provided me with security and a good income. I could work shifts and then be with my family or get away. I didn't have some of the constraints other doctors have, overseeing their patients over time, building a practice and then becoming trapped by it. But I also had challenges because I worked long shifts, including nights, holidays and weekends, and the ER is generally a very stressful place to work.

Then a very good friend died at the age of 32 from malignant melanoma. About six months before he died, when it was clear that the cancer was spreading and there wasn't any real hope of reversing it, he and his family asked me to help him through the death process. I became his primary doctor and then his hospice doctor, and our families became very close. I recognized then that I might not have as much time left as I thought, and I understood that this life was going to end. I also realized I was no longer afraid of death. My friend was an incredible teacher for me. I paid a lot of attention as he became very accepting and loving, just wanting to be with his wife and children. He died three days after 9/11. We were all in this amazing vigil of support—it was like a cocoon—and that set something in motion in me. A few months later I had an epiphany.

I was sitting on a bluff overlooking the ocean in Big Sur when I was infused by a feeling of light energy. I had an awakening that my life was meant to take a different path: "You are in control. You can choose, and you are responsible for making a great life for yourself and your family. You have everything you need to do it." I was so inspired, I filled up a pad of legal paper with a letter to myself about what I wanted, things to start doing, and how I envisioned life developing.

Even though I went back to work as an ER doctor, I knew I was on a different path, and fortunately my wife came on board too. We started learning together about different business options so we could create more choices for ourselves and have a bigger impact.

As I reflect back on my path I'm proud of each of

the business ventures I embarked on because they happened out of a desire to fill an obvious need in my community, and I wasn't afraid to go for it! I started a house call practice for seniors as well as an in-home care company to help seniors remain independent in their homes. I also started hosting a radio show on issues of importance to seniors. I assisted my wife when she opened several Curves Fitness franchises in Guam and California. When the county hospital in my town closed in 2007, the hospital I worked at decided to open an urgent care clinic, a rural health care clinic and an inpatient hospital program. As the entrepreneur of my emergency medical group, I stepped up and negotiated several contracts with the hospital. Over the next several months I helped start several practices, clinics and programs.

In 2010 I decided it was important to become a better speaker so I could be more confident and influential in the business world. A friend of mine knew Lisa, so I bought one of her programs and then ended up at her live event in San Diego in October of 2010, not really knowing what to expect. At the event, I became incredibly inspired, focused and determined. I'm a physician and scientifically trained, and I was fairly skeptical when one of her speakers, Tim Kelley, invited us to do an exercise to identify our Life Purpose, but I was also willing to open myself up to new possibilities, and I got it!

I was sitting in a room of people who were connected, and I knew at that moment I wanted to be part of something like that. I wanted to create that. I envisioned the same feeling in a room full of doctors, nurses and healthcare experts improving the health and wellbeing of the planet, coming together and sharing the same kind of energy, openness, vulnerability and inspiration.

My Life Purpose that came to me so clearly in San Diego was to help other people see the light within themselves, get beyond their fear and experience more joy and meaning in their lives—I was to be a "Doctor on Purpose."

My wife and I joined the Sassy Mastermind at the Diamond level, the first time we invested in any kind of personal coaching. Lisa's model of leveraging your passion and gifts and then creating something really phenomenal from it taught me not to be afraid of getting out there, to persevere, to really push and believe in what I'm doing.

The people who became my dearest friends in the mastermind were spiritual, interested in everybody's wellbeing, wanted to see me succeed, and offered guidance, advice, love, criticism, all of it in a genuine way. They helped me stay accountable. I've had thought leaders and business people it would be difficult to meet become my mentors and guides. Lisa's mastermind is the model for what I want to create.

Now that I've relocated to San Diego, one of the projects I'm involved with is developing a new model for a medical clinic that combines urgent care with integrative health, pain management and performance enhancement, to offer people the type of care they want and need the most. We're going to hold town hall meetings so the community can be involved in designing the health center in partnership with us.

I'm now known as "The ER Doctor for the Heart and Soul." That's how I've assumed the throne. I'm living my life aligned with my highest values, my innate gifts and my life purpose. I found a system, a way to find a high level of internal happiness and peace of mind in my own life, and now I'm teaching and coaching others to do it too.

Through my coaching and programs I help people become very clear about who they are at a very deep level—their essence—so they can design their lives in alignment with what they know to be true about themselves. I work with people both individually and in group programs, and I'm starting to work with medical practices and business teams.

Through my work, people are able to share their gifts, to come from a place of joy, and to give the best of what they have. I am a conduit for other people to live their purpose and create the most joyful, meaningful and fulfilling lives possible.

Grab your free gift from Dr. Bob Uslander
at www.MeetTheSassies.com today.

America's Wealth Mentor

by
Linda P. Jones

I grew up in a middle class home on Mercer Island, a suburb of Seattle. Because it was an island and had beautiful views and expensive waterfront property, some of my friends with wealthy parents lived in mansions on the water. I wondered how wealth grew and why some people were wealthy and others weren't. It led me to investigate wealth building, and I read *Think and Grow Rich* when I was 10 years old!

To learn more about finances, I earned a business degree at the University of Washington, became a CFP®, (Certified Financial Planner), and worked for investment firms. The last nine years of my success-ful 25-year career were as a regional vice president at one of the largest and most respected brokerage firms, representing some of the industry's top money managers in an eight-state territory with over $200 million in annual sales.

While in the investment industry, I realized how millionaires became wealthy was sometimes opposite to what is commonly believed. For example, million-aires often built wealth by concentrating their money in one asset like real estate (think Donald Trump) or a few stocks (like Warren Buffet), rather than by being broadly diversified.

By studying millionaires and how they built wealth, I was able to identify "Eight Steps to Wealth." I applied these steps to my own life, bought technology stocks during the tech bubble, made my first million dollars at age 38, and made another million the next year. From there, I realized that bubbles occur regularly in investments, and I could see real estate looming as the next bubble. I used that to my advantage to time the sale of a house at the peak of the real estate bubble.

In 2005, my husband passed away suddenly from a brain aneurysm. In my grief I knew my life would change dramatically. I felt I wasn't living my life's purpose—I was meant to teach other people what I knew about money and investing. This became clear when dealing with lawyers as the executrix of my husband's estate. I wondered how women with no financial experience would cope. I sought out mentors to help me create a business and started the Global Institute of Wealth for Women.

I knew part of my mission was to help women with handling money, and I was qualified to teach them. I felt learning about money and investing could be made more interesting for women. I would not only show them how money worked, but how to invest the way millionaires invest, teaching advanced concepts not common in the investment industry and making them easily understandable and interesting to learn.

For example, during the 2008 financial crisis, I discovered that financial cycles exist in our economy. Over 4,200 different cycles have been determined on this planet and they can even be seen in the financial markets. These cycles repeat at regular intervals, and if you understand them, you can actually see ahead to what might happen in the future in financial markets. These planetary movements were what first successfully forecasted weather patterns for almanacs and later were used by commodity investors.

An investor in the early 1900s made a $50 million fortune by studying how the planets moved in relation to one another and how that coincided with movements in the stock market. I also learned there is a correlation between the economy and sunspot cycles. In 1999, when the stock market was climbing in the tech bubble that Federal Reserve Chairman Alan Greenspan dubbed "irrational exuberance," sunspot cycles were at their highest peak. In 2008 when the stock market crashed and the economy was in a deep recession, we experienced the lowest sunspot activity in our generation. It's fascinating that there is a correlation between what's going on in the economy and what's happening on a planetary level! I only discovered this a few years ago, but some billionaires know this and have been using it successfully to their investing advantage for decades.

My style of investing and building wealth appeals to women (and smart men) because I take complex subjects and make them simple to understand. I don't use jargon or lingo when teaching about investing. One of the ways I teach others to have a "Wealthy Mindset" is to step out of fear and into gratitude.

Right now there's a lot of fear in the news. We are deluged with messages from TV and advertising that keep us in a perpetual state of fear. Fear and gratitude cannot exist in your mind at the same time. That's the easiest starting point to begin to create your own wealth. It's about being grateful for everything you have!

I joined the Sassy Mastermind at the Diamond level as a way to work with Lisa and get clear on my message and my value. She suggested I become a wealth mentor. Lisa and the mastermind really got my business going, showing me what I could successfully offer and how to do it. My new brand, Be Wealthy & Smart, was affirmed by the mastermind. The mastermind gave me confidence that people needed and wanted what I was offering. I wouldn't have a multi-six-figure business today without Lisa and the Sassy Mastermind.

Once I stepped into being America's Wealth Mentor, I planned my first three-day live event, the

"Be Wealthy & Smart Intensive: Step Into A World Of Wealth," in Palm Springs, CA in June of 2011. I wanted to share the plan that made me wealthy and that would allow women to be more comfortable with money. The mastermind was instrumental in helping me name my event and choose the content. I even selected all my speakers from the mastermind! At my event, I offered a six-month mastermind of my own, with diamond and platinum levels, and generated $120,000 that weekend, and more importantly, helped women start building wealth for themselves. The surprising twist was Lisa hired me as her wealth mentor and joined my mastermind! Thanks to Lisa and the Sassy Mastermind, today I have a thriving business.

People often ask me how I'm different from Suze Orman. There are three ways: I teach how finances move in cycles and peak in bubbles (like the tech and real estate bubbles), I teach sophisticated wealth building techniques billionaires use, and I teach the "Eight Steps to Wealth," the way millionaires create wealth quickly.

I also start with your wealthy mindset, because many women think money is a bad thing, or it's wrong to want it, or they are not worthy and deserving of wealth, or they can't be spiritual and have money. When women improve their relationship to money, they help others and do great works. I suggest using your gifts, talents and passions, what I call your "personal currency." If you use your personal currency to make a living, you are likely to become very successful and also enjoy what you do.

The Dalai Lama said the Western woman will save the world. I think that's because as Western women become entrepreneurs and acquire wealth, they are giving money to the poor and suffering—and eventually the whole planet will be changed.

Grab your free gift from Linda P. Jones
at www.MeetTheSassies.com today.

> "People aren't actually saying 'yes' to you, they are saying 'yes' to themselves, to their own transformation."
>
> —Lisa Sasevich

Chapter Five

The Magic of Taking Inspired Action

Listen, Act, Trust

Listen: The Tap or the 2 x 4

Many times we get a little intuition, an inkling about what we should move forward with. "I should call that person." "I should buy that gift." "I should contribute to that foundation." "I should take a nap." But we don't act on it—we second-guess ourselves and we ignore that little tap on our shoulder. Where does it come from? It depends on your beliefs: God, Source, your intuition, your Higher Self—you decide. We can all agree that there is some force that is informing us that is outside of our mental capacity, and when we learn to tap in and listen to it, magical things happen.

Part of Living Sassy is to start opening your level of awareness and pay attention to the little taps. The key is to act on them as quickly as you can and then to trust the actions that you take. This is important because you can waste a lot of time second-guessing yourself and wondering why you took a certain action. But if you take the route of trusting and know that if you stay aware, you'll either discover directly, or from another source, what that inspiration was all about. When I look back at the magical times in my life and the things that have helped me the most, it's when I had a small thought, I took an action, and it turned into something that was transformational for me or for someone else.

An example of this would be when I had the thought to contact the eWomenNetwork (which is a network of businesswomen nearly one million strong) to make a contribution to their members. The network provides information and support to businesswomen. The foundation arm of eWomen is a nonprofit that gives grants and awards to women and children, as well as recognition for promising young women in their Emerging Leaders program. They also help with natural disasters, creating homes for veterans and other charitable causes.

> If you don't listen to the taps, be careful because you might get the 2 x 4

I'd thought of contacting them for many years, but one day I was sitting at my computer and it actually occurred to me to "do it now." I wrote a letter, and within an hour I had a response from the founder of the company saying that what I had sounded amazing and they wanted me to be the keynote speaker at their upcoming conference with thousands of women in attendance.

This is an opportunity that many people would angle for over the course of many years, but because I followed the taps, in one e-mail, I was in direct conversation with the head of the organization. We ended up building a relationship that inspired me to raise donations totaling hundreds of thousands of dollars for their foundation, and later resulted in hundreds of thousands of dollars for my business by speaking from their stage. It was a career-changer, and it would not have happened had I not listened to the tap, acted, and then trusted that action.

Listen, Act, Trust

Act: What Happens if You Don't Listen to the Taps?

There will be times in your life when you get a tap—and you still have free will—so you may or may not decide to honor it. But I can tell you, and I've heard that Oprah said something similar on one of her shows, if you don't listen to the taps, be careful because you might get the 2 x 4. If there is something that Spirit is really wanting from you and you are not willing to listen to the little hints that come along the way, it is common that you will get slapped right on the forehead because your attention was not obtained with a small tickle. Some of you may have heard this described as "First God throws pebbles, then He throws stones, then comes the boulder . . . "

So I invite you to think about an area of your life where you got the small tickle and you didn't pay attention, and it took the 2 x 4 to really get to you. An area of my own life would be my health. I've always been so vibrant and healthy. But I got the tap about a year ago while I was sitting at in seminar that suggested testing my mercury levels and my adrenals. It came listening to the speaker who happened to be one of my Sassies. I followed the tap and got the test, and found out that both areas were in the danger zone, and I really needed to do some work on my health. I hired an expert and did what they said, but only to a certain degree.

Within months I found myself extremely tired and on the verge of adrenal burnout, which could have left me on the couch, unable to function. The 2 x 4 was right around the corner. I took the second set of tests after only half following the expert's orders. The test results were frighteningly low and it was clear that I was at risk of adrenal burnout and not being able to function. With a five and eight-year old at home, that was not an option. So I decided to have those test results be the 2 x 4 instead of having another wake-up call that would put me out of commission. It didn't take becoming completely immobilized for me to listen.

Listen, Act, Trust

Trust: Stand Firm, Stay Open

After you've listened and taken action you might feel somewhat vulnerable. That's the time when other people may judge what you did. I remember when I made the choice to register for a mastermind program that cost $100,000 for a year of coaching. My accountant, my friends and other people in my life all thought I was crazy. I had infants at home, a husband in medical residency, and had barely made that much money ever in a whole year! I learned from that experience that there are two things to do after you have trusted the tap and acted.

Number one: stand firm. Trust that you took that action because of the tap that you got. It wasn't random, and while nobody else may have gotten the tap, and nobody else was in on that unique experience that made you act that way, you were—and that's all that matters.

Number two: at the same time, you need to stay open. After you listen and take that action, you need to stand firm in your choice. But you also want to stay open because at that point you may get an additional bit of information, an additional tap for the next thing to do. You want to stand firm but not closed. You want to stand firm and stay open.

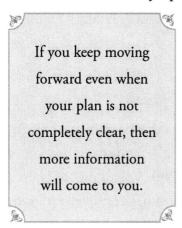

If you keep moving forward even when your plan is not completely clear, then more information will come to you.

I'm thanking God that I did stay open because even after investing $100,000 in myself to transform my business, other mentors showed up along the way. It was hard to for me to believe that I would have to pay anyone else after that kind of investment, but I did.

The first investment I ever made in myself was $3,000 for a workshop about taking your business to the next level. I had to scrape up the money to go. It was six months away, but before it rolled around I invested another $7,500 in a different course. I stayed open, I listened and I took action on what felt right, and in that year my business skyrocketed from $130,000 in sales to over two million dollars. I am always on the lookout for new opportunities to learn, and always listening for the next tap to up-level personally and professionally.

I shared one of my favorite quotes in Chapter One from Maxwell Maltz. You need to be moving forward in order for Source to correct you on your path. Like that parked car, it's impossible to move the wheels when

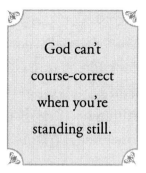

God can't course-correct when you're standing still.

it's not rolling, but the minute it's moving forward, the automatic steering kicks in and it's easy to navigate. It's the same with your life and it's a part of Living Sassy.

If you keep moving forward even when your plan is not completely clear, even if you move toward what you *think your plan is, what your dime appears to be* and *the best information you can pick up from that tap you received*, then more information and inspiration will likely come to you. When you're standing still you are stagnant. It's a lot like a pond vs. a river. If a pond doesn't have a spring flowing through it, it stagnates. So do people if they don't keep moving forward.

Heart vs. Head

This may be one of the biggest mindset shifts for those of you out there selling your products and services, especially in situations where you're looking for a client to make a decision on the spot. Part of Living Sassy is realizing that in order to make big money doing what you love and getting your gifts out into the world, you need people to say "yes." However, they aren't actually saying "yes" to you, although it may look like it on the outside, they are really saying "yes" to themselves, to their own transformation and to the difference they want to make in their own lives, their own relationships and businesses.

It's common to think that when presented with an opportunity that could transform their lives (the opportunities that you present to them), people should have "time to sleep on it," and that if they're given that time to sleep on it, that's the only way they're going to come up with the "sane decision" or a "good decision." The truth is when someone is given time to "think" about it, they're doing just what it says—going to their head for answers. Unfortunately our head is not the place that necessarily gives us the best guidance. Presented with an opportunity, the truth is that our heart "knows." Our heart leaps if it's something we're supposed to do; although of course we may still feel a pang of anxiety or some fear coming in because it's such a risk and a big opportunity.

You use your head to think things through but it does not always have the most empowering opinion about you: "You know, I took an opportunity, I took a leap like this before, and I didn't follow through, so what makes me think I'll follow through this time?" Or "Those results may work for those other people but I doubt they would work for me." Then there's "I don't have the money, I should wait." And "I don't have the time right now." That's small thinking. Someone could be sitting in your audience a year from now and use the same excuses. Will they have time a year from now? Will they have the money then? They could waste an entire year with these excuses. If they use those indicators to stop them, their lives will never move forward.

In the classic children's book *The Little Me and the Great Me* by Lou Austin[5] that I read to my own kids, the author asserts that we have a Great Me and a Little Me. The Great Me is the one who is making higher choices, and, I would venture to say, the one who looks out for your best interests—and that's your heart. The Little Me is contracted and small, it's scared, and it's trying to protect you—this one doesn't want to take risks to change your life for the better.

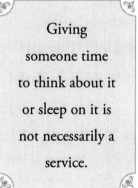

Giving someone time to think about it or sleep on it is not necessarily a service.

What I recommend to my kids comes from that book. When you get stuck in the Little Me, you take a deep breath and you blow the Little Me right out and then you inhale the Great Me. Sometimes that's what you have to do when you're faced

---

5   Lou Austin, *The Little Me and the Great Me* (Partnership Foundation, 1957).

with a decision that could really change your life. And that's what you have to be willing to let your clients do. So giving someone time to think about it or sleep on it is not necessarily a service. In fact, what you're doing is you're giving them the chance to go from their heart, which knows the right action to take, into their head, where they talk themselves out of the thing that could really transform their lives.

So get some practice with making offers. We will explore inspiring others to take on-the-spot action in the third section of this book. But for right now it's important to get comfortable with making offers and get comfortable with allowing people to move through their own discomfort on the way to saying "yes." In your own decision-making process, if you're looking for things to be comfortable and convenient, you are using the wrong scale. Living Sassy has to do with being willing to be uncomfortable by doing what is inconvenient in order to make a big difference and big money doing what you love.

You Can't Out-Give God

If there's one thing I've learned in a beautiful way over the last few years it's that you can't out-give God. I read a book by Edwene Gaines called *The Four Spiritual Laws Of Prosperity*[6] where she introduces the

---

6   Edwene Gaines, *The Four Spiritual Laws of Prosperity* (Holtzbrinck Publishers, 2005).

idea of tithing. By her definition, tithing is giving 10% of all the money that comes your way to a person, place or institution that feeds you spiritual food or reminds you of who you are. She invited us to take it on as a six-month experiment, which I did, fully expecting that if it didn't work I would just stop.

Four years later it is at the top of my list of my spiritual practices. I credit it for providing me with the wonderful and abundant life that I enjoy. In fact, one of the things that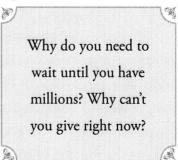

Why do you need to wait until you have millions? Why can't you give right now?

the Sassy program proposes is that you can't out-give God, and this has come true in my life so many times I can't even count them all. I'll send out a $3,000 check to someone who inspired me, and I'll open my mailbox and there will be a $3,500 refund from the IRS that I wasn't expecting.

One of my clients said, "The most exciting thing for me about tithing is that I wanted this to be the year that I started a scholarship program I've been wanting to do. I have these thoughts that one day when I have millions, I'll be able to donate millions and really create a school and blah-blah-blah. And it occurred to me, why do you need to wait until you have millions? Why can't you give $500 right now? The thought of tithing has always been there. I've done it loosely but I decided to take up that challenge and put 10% of every single dollar that came in into a special fund right then, and it has made it so exciting. It makes me realize constantly the spiritual food that I'm receiving and how I can tithe back to that. It's created an excitement in me that really helps me recognize that I'm living my purpose."

Tithing in action came about when I went to speak at the eWomenNetwork foundation stage—I shared with you earlier about them and how I took inspired action when I contacted them. When I went to speak, I was surprised to be acknowledged by them as their Femtor of the Year Foundation Champion for having raised so much money for their foundation. Every year eWomen gives out International Femtor Awards. Over the course of two of my large events, my audience and I raised over $250,000. As spirit would have it, when I went to speak there they gave me the opportunity to offer my services in the back of the room, which is something that I teach other people how to do, so it was really a pleasure. You will never guess how much money we made from the sales of our products. That's right—just over $250,000. Once again it was proven to me that you can't out-give God.

Starting the
Soul Sitter Movement

by
Stacey Canfield

L isa invited me to photograph her very first Sassy retreat in January 2010 at the Miraval Resort in Arizona, introducing me to 30 wonderful Sassies. As I drove through the desert, I found myself reflecting on my Aunt Mary who had lived in Arizona. She was my godmother, and I took care of her 18 months earlier as she died of cancer. All of a sudden out of the blue I heard her voice saying, "You are here to help people die."

It stopped me cold. I said, "Aunt Mary?"

I was so caught off guard and I wondered if this was a sign, so I said, "Okay Universe, bring it. If I heard this right, give me a sign."

About 100 yards in front of me out of nowhere I saw a graveyard. Cactus and tumbleweeds for miles and then this. That was my sign. "All right, God. It's just you and me for the next four days at Miraval. I'm ready for whatever you're going to show me."

At this lovely high-end, five-star resort, I'm told there's an intuitive on site with one more psychic reading left. It's $300, so I decline. Hauling my photo equipment into my room, I heard Aunt Mary's voice say, "This is why you're here."

An hour later, the psychic told me she's getting a strong female presence in the room who wants to thank me for being with her while she died. Four family members were a mother to me in some way and I affectionately call them my "Mother Guides" because I was with them when they took their final breaths. I told the psychic about the voice I heard and she said, "This is your mission. I see you speaking before groups, and helping people die. I see you coming up with the tools and the language so people will know what it's like to be with dying people and see the grace and the ease of how you do it. You're going to share it with the world. It is so needed in this time of the shift."

I could feel the weight of this, as if I were being knocked over. There I was, just a photographer who has never studied a stitch of medicine, I didn't care take for a living, I wasn't a nurse. (Although nothing scares me, I'm very, very comfortable with the death process.)

I stumbled out of the session and ran into Lisa. I told her I thought my life just changed. She smiled as if she knew I was in the right place at the right time. I don't know what I would have done without Lisa. She provided a safe place for me to be able to conceptualize what this could look like and gave me the possibility that I could take something so profound and something so much bigger than myself and turn it into a concrete offering to give the world.

Everything in my life prepared me for that moment. Not just spending the time with my Mother Guides, but being an entrepreneur and running a photo business for 20 years with my husband. I could remember times when we'd receive panicked phone calls at 2:00 in the morning saying, "My brother-in-law just got hit by a car and we need his picture," or someone asking for photos of a teen who had been abducted.

My photography provides legacies for people in their everyday lives, and teaching people to be Soul Sitters preserves that legacy, makes it possible for people to hand it down. It's a way for people to say goodbye to their lives while being conscious of what they leave behind. I help create dialogue with a program called The Passage Plan to communicate the wants, needs and wishes a person has when it's time to cross over.

The Passage Plan is likened to an emotional and spiritual will. Most of us have a will drafted by our lawyers that helps us decide what to do with all the material things we leave behind. The Passage Plan is the missing spiritual piece that helps families care for their loved ones as they are dying. How many times do people say, "I don't know what to do?" The Passage Plan fills that void of uncertainty so they can follow the dying person's wishes.

I did take inspired action to start Soul Sitters, but I couldn't go forward with it if I was just focused on the money. I know the money will come but it's important to keep the mission bigger than the money. I wanted to keep the Soul Sitter website free for anyone who needed it, so I created a website that is full of articles, stories and resources for people facing losing a loved one. The resources on Soul Sitters will remain, so in order to sustain it, I created the Passage Plan, which will also become a web application.

The beauty of the Passage Plan is that it can be updated any time. It will have a membership-based application and I will offer a variety of classes that will teach people how to complete their plan. Since Soul Sitters teaches people how to be present for a dying loved one, why not prepare a plan for what you may want for yourself one day? Let's face it, we are all going to die, why not request what kind of music you want playing in your final hours? My ideal clients are healthy baby boomers who have experienced their own loss and want to leave behind a more positive dying experience for their own family members.

The Passage Plan is broken down into five parts called the TABLE of Contents because it's the acronym T.A.B.L.E.

T, the first part, is assigning one's **Tribe of** all the significant people wanted by the ailing person, with an assigned contact person to reach them and to start the energy of prayer, whether for a great recovery or a peaceful passing.

A, the second part, is **Affirming** and **Amending**, with a beautiful forgiveness packet.

B is **Beliefs**, outlining religious or spiritual beliefs and who will be chosen to give spiritual counseling.

L is the **Legacy** component to help people dream about what they want to leave behind. It gives people the opportunity to think big.

E is **Environment**. The physical environment at death is about music, books, journaling tools and options such as dying in a home or hospice facility, who will read them their favorite books, do they want to hear a live piano, pet a cat or have access to a window to see outside.

Soul Sitters help prepare people to cross over. By creating a Passage Plan, a family is trained to be Soul Sitters. Part of their journey is to think about their soul's responsibility for the energy they leave behind on earth. Can you imagine a time where all that remains is a more positive and beautiful world full of loving energy, powerful enough to heal the planet? That's my goal.

Being a Sassy has given me a safe place to dream and a nurturing environment of smart people willing to take risks and take inspired action. It's invigorating to be around like-minded people who want to make positive changes in the world. For the longest time I wondered how the heck could I make money at this? The Sassies can see the vision. Even when I can't see it myself, they can see it for me.

I told Lisa she was the biggest surprise of my life. It was nothing I sought after. She showed up and she never sold me, I never felt pitched to, and my life has changed so much by joining the Sassy Mastermind. She started out supporting my photography business and now she's supporting bringing really huge ideas like Soul Sitters and the Passage Plan into the world. I don't think the Passage Plan would be here without Lisa.

Grab your free gift from Stacey Canfield
at www.MeetTheSassies.com today.

Choosing to Live and Taking Others With Me

by
Joyce O'Brien

My husband and I thought we were living the dream life with successful careers, building a new home and starting a family. Then in a five-year period of time, a series of unimaginable events ultimately led me to taking the most inspired action I ever imagined possible.

It all began one sunny spring day when I was working on Wall Street. I got a call from my husband, Kevin. I could hardly recognize his voice. He said he was a little numb. As it turned out he'd actually had a brain hemorrhage, and his whole right side was paralyzed.

A year later, I was pregnant and the doctors thought our baby had Spina bifida and advised discontinuing the pregnancy. We listened to our hearts and decided whatever happened, we would all be okay.

After our daughter was born, I went back to work and was promoted to a high-level executive position running a successful $2.1 billion business. I was feeling awkward in my post-pregnancy body, so I decided to have some suits made to fit my new body.

I "accidentally" found a local suit designer in the yellow pages.

Shortly after meeting with her, when my daughter was just eight months old, I was diagnosed with Stage IIB breast cancer. I lost everything—my disability, life and health insurance, and my Wall Street career. I called the suit designer and told her I wouldn't need my suits for a while. She told me to contact the holistic practitioners who helped her when she was ill. I didn't listen to this "tap" and underwent a mastectomy and chemotherapy. I did call the practitioners after my surgery, but they sounded too far out there, so I let it go.

A year after that, my husband was diagnosed with stage IIIB malignant melanoma and given a 20%-30% chance of survival.

Even though the whispers became louder and louder, I still hadn't listened and returned to Wall Street. That's when the most shocking news of all came … I had a recurrence—stage IV terminal cancer. I got down on my knees and I begged God for help. We had a baby, we were in our mid 30s and were likely going to die. The first guidance that popped into my head was to call the far-out holistic practitioners.

When I went to see them, I didn't only have cancer. For years, I'd been living with chronic fatigue, sinus problems, headaches, migraines, depression and irritable bowel syndrome. When I began healing holistically, all of those symptoms disappeared within 30 days and I felt fantastic. I had never felt better in my life.

Those symptoms had been giving me messages and I wasn't listening.

I'd come to discover that we're meant to feel fantastic, and in order to truly heal cancer or any physical health condition, we need to heal physically, mentally, emotionally and spiritually; including emotional traumas from childhood.

The good news is that my husband Kevin is walking, our daughter is perfectly healthy and Kevin and I have been cancer free for over eleven years.

I knew I had to show others how they could also heal. So I took more inspired action and gave up my career on Wall Street to study holistic healing and the modalities I used to heal. I became certified as a biological practitioner, helping people get to the root of their health issues and heal physically, mentally, emotionally and spiritually. When I began sharing my story, people would tell me I had to write a book. I would say, "I'm not a writer!" At one event I attended, something propelled me to take inspired action and I said to the presenter, "I would love to take a picture with you because I want to speak on your stage." Two months later I spoke on his stage. That man was T. Harv Eker.

During that time my dad was diagnosed with cancer.

We met a woman in the next hospital room ravaged by cancer. She was even younger than I. That rocked me to my core. I kept hearing this voice saying, "Get your book written." I had no doubt it was God and I kept brushing it off saying, "I don't want to hear it, I'm not a writer." When I returned home that night I received an e-mail from a client saying, "I just want to thank you. You're my guardian angel ... you saved my life ... I feel better than I've ever felt before. **SO GO GET YOUR BOOK WRITTEN!**" When I saw that in bold capital letters after hearing it all day so loudly, it was the last push I needed.

Around that time, I was invited to one of Lisa's events and when the Sassy Mastermind was offered I "listened" to my intuition, which lifted me out of my seat to sign up without hesitation! I knew I needed to be a part of it, to be with a group of like-minded people. It felt like home. Before Sassy, I felt I was alone, doing it all on my own. Once I joined the Sassies, I quickly made lifelong friends who were just as excited about my successes as they were about their own. They wanted to support me in creating an amazing business.

After joining the mastermind, I published my book *Choose to Live* and it quickly became a number one bestseller. I've created my signature talk and gotten wonderful opportunities to speak on Lisa's stage several times—giving me a whole new confidence level in my speaking abilities. By combining what I learned from Lisa with the confidence, guidance, support and structure that Lisa provided, I began to receive amazing opportunities to speak and serve clients in a much bigger way. As a result, I've shared the stage with Lisa Nichols, Jack Canfield, Les Brown, Kevin Trudeau, Marcia Wieder and more, and I've spoken at eWomen-Network's National Conference.

Lisa lays everything out for speaking as well as using strategy sessions to learn how to best serve your clients. As a result I have a high sign-up rate of 80-90% for my clients and programs. The strategy session process has brought me deep and meaningful connections. In those sessions, I can truly understand how to fulfill my client's needs and what kind of support they require to have amazing results.

There is one more piece to this story: "You Can't Out-Give God." While at Lisa's live event with my husband, we saw a video shown by eWomenNetwork's Sandra and Kym Yancey. Sandra and Kym are amazing people with tremendous hearts and the work they are doing for women entrepreneurs and through their foundation stopped us in our tracks. Two specific clips of their foundation video floored us.

One was about a policeman adopting abandoned babies to give them a family name and a proper burial. Our second child was adopted, so that was powerful for us. The second clip was of the Jack and Jill Foundation, which offers one final weekend of memories with a family member dying from cancer.

Watching this video all I could think was: that would have been us if I had not taken inspired action! I was bawling, my husband was bawling, and we decided to make a donation, with no expectations of receiving anything in return. We did it with tremendous gratitude for the gift of life that we had already been given.

Since you can't out-give God, shortly after Lisa's event, I was given a tremendous speaking opportunity and separately we received an unexpected check in the exact amount we had donated. Later, after another tithe, we learned about a pension plan from Kevin's former employer. They had been holding onto it for 18 years, unable to find him. We had money appearing out of nowhere!

At Lisa's event I became very clear that I was here to shift the health of the planet—that's my big mission. I could never go back to my old way of life. My healing journey, being willing to transform my life, taking inspired action and becoming a Sassy have opened so many unexpected doors, created cherished friendships and are among the greatest blessings of my life.

Grab your free gift from Joyce O'Brien
at www.MeetTheSassies.com today.

When God Says Go

by
Crystal Gifford

I am the founder of The Empowered Wealth Network where I empower purpose-driven entrepreneurs who are looking to live guilt-free, sustainable lives of luxury by mastering their finances and creating a path to enjoy life now and through retirement.

I resonated with Lisa because she is authentic, spiritual, and has the systems my business needs. My inspired journey started when I was drawn to attend one of Lisa's live events and felt like I needed to go, but it wasn't a good time. I had just invested heavily to get my business going, but I was so drawn to the event it kept me up at night. So when I received a refund check for $200 unexpectedly, I told God if he really wanted me go, he would show me by providing the other $800. Not long after that, I found a check that somehow was forgotten for six weeks, and it was for $842! That was my clear indication to go to the event. Then as I booked the event, a friend who had already registered offered me a half-price guest ticket!

During the event there was an opportunity to tithe to the Jenna Druck Foundation. Something about this organization drew me, but I didn't know how much to give, so I requested a day's extension to figure that out.

The next morning while running it became clear that I needed to give $720. In my mind I saw myself writing a check for that amount. I wrestled with this number, but by the end of the jog I resolved to give that amount. I committed myself wholeheartedly to giving even though I did not fully understand why. One thing I have learned through my Sassy experience already is we give from our hearts and not our heads. This is our opportunity to give freely, release into the universe, and open ourselves to whatever is in store for us through our generosity. When I was ready to write the check, I realized I hadn't brought my emergency fund checks—the only source of funds I had free at the time.

I felt frustrated. Here I am, I'm willing to give, and I can't access the money. I asked God, "Why put this on me?" I felt something nudging me to check my accounts. I argued. I knew there was hardly enough in my account to cover $720 so I ignored it. But again came the nudging, this time like a voice in my head, "Check your accounts." The third time the prompting was bolder and more demanding.

By the third time God speaks, I pay attention. More to prove God wrong than to actually check my accounts with expectation, I went on my computer. To my surprise, the money was there! I had recently completed a contract for a client who was making payments. There was an unexpected $1500 in my account. I laughed at myself for being so stubborn and for taking so long to look. The way this all worked out was amazing!

I've always been an entrepreneur at heart, trying to get my business going for quite some time. I was teaching finance courses full-time at a university, driving two hours each way, and building my business in my spare time. I didn't have the structure in place at all. When I got the nudge "Join the Sassy Mastermind," I said,"Are you kidding me? Where am I going to come up with that money?"

Joining Sassy seemed like a good idea "someday" but joining now made no logical sense to a financial planner who teaches people to follow the principles of spending wisely and follows them herself. I didn't know how I was going to do it, but I knew in my gut that I was supposed to join. When I would say to myself, "No, I'm waiting," I would feel sick in my stomach. When I would say, "Yes, I am doing it," I was completely enveloped in peace beyond my own understanding. I chose to go with my gut over my head on this one.

Once I made the final decision, all the pieces made sense and suddenly I began to understand the value of this choice not as "spending" but an "investment" in myself and in my business. This realization made me feel lighter and more serene. Well, the money all came together the day before the funds were due. Everything processed and went through and I had the cash to pay in full for the mastermind.

I had no idea what this would mean for my business, but once I joined all the systems started to fall into place. Lisa's step-by-step formulas make so much sense and the contacts I'm making are incredible. I'm considering a potential partnership with a Sassy alumnus to bring our two areas of expertise in finance together. We plan to pair up for some joint speaking engagements where we can build off each other's energy. So many opportunities have opened up from being a Sassy.

As if to say, "I told you this is what I want for you", God once again delivered an unexpected, positive shift in my life. Right after I joined the mastermind, I received a job offer for a full-time position to be part of the Kaplan University online finance faculty, which meant I would be working from home! With the commute gone, I was able to put all my other plans in place. I've captured 15 to 20 hours a week in driving time alone that I can devote to my business.

I earned my Certified Financial Planner™ designation with the intention to complete financial plans for my clients and offer some finance products when appropriate, but this has turned into a much bigger vision. Since I've become a Sassy, it's gone from this idea of "I can do this on the side" to "This is what my life is about." I am now where I should be, and all the years of teaching have prepared me to work in groups, leverage my expertise, and speak confidently to large groups.

I get to help people remove all the obstacles to their dreams and to put financial systems in place to achieve those dreams. Financial barriers are one major obstacle that holds so many people back. If we can get that taken care of, anything can become real. I'm not just setting people up financially, I'm opening up possibilities in their lives and helping them learn to embrace their money to enjoy life now *and* in their future.

After all the guidance I received that led me to become a Sassy, I know if people take guided steps their dreams will become real. At the closing of one of our Sassy retreats, we recited the prayer of Abundantia, the Goddess of Prosperity. It includes the words:

"… Help me replace any money worries with joy and gratitude. Help me open my arms so that Heaven may easily help me … I'm truly grateful, and I'm abundantly joyful and fulfilled. I let go, and relax in the sure knowledge that I'm completely taken care of, immediately and in the future."

If I can provide this liberation for my clients, then I know I have reached my purpose.

Grab your free gift from Crystal Gifford
at <u>www.MeetTheSassies.com</u> today.

Chapter Six

Be the Client You Want to Attract

L iving Sassy is about having the right mindset, being conscious of the fact that how you act in the world gets mirrored back to you. Did you ever notice how your clients have the same issues you do? Or that what's hardest for them can be the most difficult thing for you? One place this shows up is in the area of sales. I often share my belief that you can't expect people to invest in themselves through you at a level greater than you've invested in yourself.

I had a client call me to talk about doing a VIP day with me. She spoke about all the work she wanted to get done together. We created the perfect package for her based on her problem, which was that she just wasn't getting people to say "yes" to her. And then, at the end of the day she left thinking about it. That's a perfect example. Her would-be clients are all leaving her "thinking about it" too. If that's what you're doing, that's what you're going to get. I call it Business Karma. What you're putting out is likely what you're seeing. So if you don't like what you're seeing, if you get a lot of people looking for the best price, or thinking about it, or vacillating, or not taking action, look at what you're doing yourself. The good news is that you can change it. Start taking action, and so will your clients. Start investing in yourself, and so will your clients.

> I would never have thought of selling $3,000 programs until I opened the door by investing in myself at that level.

The first time I decided to invest in myself was for the $3,000 workshop I mentioned in Chapter Five. I had taken my business as far as it could go—to $130,000 a year—by listening to expert's free calls and teleclasses, trading advice with people, paying attention to different marketing campaigns and reading books. But I could not take on one more client. I didn't have the time, my kids were one and three years old and I was the breadwinner. I was frustrated because I'd been stuck at six figures for many years. So I took the plunge when they offered a payment option, $500 each month until the workshop began in six months.

This was the first time I invested a big chunk of money into my "blessing," my own business, and it completely transformed the way I felt about myself from that time forward. I started selling VIP days for $3,000, and I sold eight of them very quickly. I would never have thought of selling $3,000 programs until I opened the door by investing in myself at that level.

Then I took some of the money I made and invested it in another course—a $7,500 course. Within three weeks of starting that course, I was selling a $7,500 program. By making that investment, I knew it was possible and easy for someone to see they needed what I had to offer, and to dig deep to pay for it, because I had done that.

When I finally made it to the $3,000 workshop, they made an offer at the end for a yearlong mentorship program with a $20,000 level and a $100,000 level. I didn't think I'd be responding to the offer, but there I was sitting in the audience calculating that the $3,000 investment had earned me $24,000. And the $7,500 investment brought in over $30,000. All I could think was: "What would happen if I made a $100,000 investment in myself?"

Then Great Me and Little Me had a bit of a battle. Great Me wanted to scream, "Yes!" And Little Me was saying, "You can't, it's crazy, what about the kids? You don't have the money . . . " Seven months after I signed up for the $100,000 mastermind, I started enrolling clients in $100,000 programs of my own, and I am the market leader in result-producing high-ticket mastermind programs today.

The bottom line is: If you want people refunding from your programs, ask for a refund. If you want people saying, "I'll think about it," go think about it. If you want decisive clients, be decisive. If you want clients to invest, invest in yourself.

 In addition to what I've shared with you here, I've prepared a bonus training for you on something I call "Business Karma." You can access it here at www.Sassy21DayChallenge.com.

How Betting On Myself Paid Off

by
Pamela Bruner

B efore I became a Sassy, I had been interested in Lisa for some time. I'd heard a lot about her but I'd never seen her live until attending one of her events in 2010. It was a life-changing experience for me because I was working very hard on my business, yet starting to feel I was not really answering the call of my heart. I was moving away from the love of what I did, and that perfect resonance that comes when you work on what you are meant to do. When I saw Lisa, she was an example of being very clear, coming from her heart and achieving great success, all at the same time. I admired that and I wanted to emulate it.

I was already committed to working with another coach for the next year, a coach I respected and wanted to work with, and I wanted to work with Lisa too, at the Diamond level, so I signed up with her as well. I had two coaches that year. It's not something I recommend for people who aren't at a certain level in their business because you don't want to get too much input when you are just starting out—it can be confusing. I was at the level where I could benefit from advice from both coaches from very different directions, and I felt Lisa could provide an essential part, which she did. I ended up investing around $175,000 that year in coaching, but it was the first year I made a million dollars, so I had a great return on my investment!

I was nervous because, like most people, I don't drop hundreds of thousands of dollars without thinking about it. Taking that big step was scary but it also felt like the right thing to do. There are times when you just need to step up, when you need to offer yourself support for where you're going, not just for where you are.

During that year I kept calling Lisa my "personal growth coach" because there was a lot I learned in her group about who I wanted to be in addition to what I wanted to do. One of the things I recognized about myself was that I tended to make snap judgments about people, what they thought about me, and what they felt about me. As I moved in bigger and bigger circles, I could not continue to do that and have successful results. I had to learn how to make up different things about what people were thinking, such as, "they love me and they want to talk to me." Since that is actually part of the work I do for with clients, it is very congruent for me to do this work personally. The way Lisa's mastermind was constructed gave me a great opportunity to work on myself, and my business is an outgrowth of me. We teach what we learn, so that's another way we can be the client we want to attract, because we work on the same issues our clients have.

I found Lisa's training to be top-notch. She has some of the best systems I've ever seen for explaining what you need to do in your business: they are clear and well laid-out, step-by-step. Having these not only helps me in my business, but also gives me the language to help me talk more effectively with my clients.

I've been coaching people for over seven years now. I've had my current business for over three years. I am a business success coach and an expert in EFT (Emotional Freedom Techniques). I specialize in helping people I call "transformational entrepreneurs" overcome their fears of sales and marketing. I do this on many levels; I have products, I have group programs, and I have high-level coaching programs. I love working with businesses at all levels of development. I had my first 3-day live event last year with 181 people in attendance, which was quite successful. This year I am co-authoring the book *Tapping Into Ultimate Success* with Jack Canfield, published by Hay House. We're launching a program to go with the book.

Recently I was scheduling a VIP day with a coach for some expertise I needed. I found it funny when he asked me, "What's your budget?" I looked at him and said, "I don't do things that way. I determine what I need for my business and then I figure out how I'm going to afford it." I've never said, "I can only do this much because this is all I can afford."

Certainly that route has taken me into debt, but it has also taken me way back out of debt. I am a firm believer in investing what you need to in your business. I find you get the returns when you take the risks, when you step up and get the support you need, whether that is support from a coach, additional training, personal growth work, or additional technology. You have to step up and get the tools you need to do your business.

So how does that relate to being the client you want to attract? I am also a client for many people. I am a client of my business manager, I am a client of my coach, I am a client of my graphic artist. I am a client who says, "This is what I need, what will it cost me?" And then I go figure out a way to afford it. When a client does that with me, I love it because I know I have a player on my hands, I'm working with someone who is really committed to success.

Being in Lisa's mastermind has been a great opportunity to work on my mindset as well as my business. Getting to know the Sassies and feeling that there are people out there who really care about my success has brought me such a sense of community. It's been a wonderful experience and I'm grateful for it.

Grab your free gift from Pamela Bruner at <u>www.MeetTheSassies.com</u> today.

How I Created Peaceful, Part-Time Prosperity

by
Lisa Cherney

Toward the end of 2008 I had a dark night of the business soul. I returned to my business semi-full-time after being on maternity leave. My daughter was 2 ½ years old and just starting preschool. I looked in the mirror one day and asked myself what was going on with my business. The spice, the enthusiasm and the big money seemed to be gone . . .

That was ironic, as my business is called Conscious Marketing and I am known as an expert at helping people market themselves by highlighting what is unique about them and bringing that out in their marketing messages. I also help them zero in on who their ideal clients are. Part of my problem was not knowing who this was anymore. I was down to $1100. I'd had my business for eight years and this was my first financial crisis. This was right when everyone started talking about the economy, and I started to buy into it.

Then I heard Lisa Sasevich on a teleclass. She made an offer for a $500 class about selling when speaking. I knew I loved to speak, and if I could get even better at attracting clients that way, I could turn things around. I took the plunge. It was completely counterintuitive to invest in something when I felt I didn't have the money, but doing just that continued to serve me as I reshaped my business.

After Lisa's course, I wanted her to see my work and tell me if I was on the right track. At the time, she was charging $2000 for three hours with her. When she told me that, I had two reactions. One was "Oh my gosh, that's a lot of money," and the other was "Good for her! She's really charging what she's worth."

I found "the money I didn't have," put it on a credit card, and met with her. This was so in alignment with "being the client you want to attract" because the clients I want to attract really go with their gut, and my gut was saying I needed to learn from Lisa. My time with Lisa was a pivotal experience that turned my business around. Lisa did for me what I do for other people—she saw my blind spots. My business was rebranded and I became The Juicy Marketing Expert. My group program became Stand Out and Be Juicy: Magnetize Your Marketing Blueprint Program, offered at $1997. It was so exciting I think I was squealing.

My new juicy program was based on a home study course I sold for $397. Lisa picked up my beautiful package of CDs and my workbook and said, "You are not going to be selling your program like this anymore. Get rid of these." I would be working with groups over the phone and charging more for it: they'd get to ask questions, receive feedback on their work, and move their businesses toward success more quickly.

Within six weeks 11 people signed up for my $1997 course. I made my money back and then some. I started noticing what happened when I invested in myself; every time I did it, I up-leveled my business. I had made $22,000 in two months—more than I earned in the second half of 2008.

A few months later Lisa and her then-business partner offered a yearlong mastermind. I had never done anything like that but I knew it was for me, even though I didn't have the $20,000. What terrified me even more than spending $20,000 was going home without the support of Lisa and the group. I didn't want to continue to "go at it alone." Since I spent all my time being the expert with the answers, I decided I needed my own expert advice and continued support. I found the money and made the investment.

In that mastermind, I decided my ultimate goal was creating my own year-long program at $20,000, which, when I started, was way far out of my realm of possibility. What could I offer that would be worth that much? How could I even say that number? Part of being the client you want to attract is being mentored by people who are attracting $20,000 clients as well, so you can experience how they do it and get accustomed to it, to the point where $20,000 feels normal.

That first year, 2009, I tripled my income to $250,000 working part-time attracting people wanting to create a business they love. I was walking my talk. The next year I launched that yearlong mentorship program. I never could have done that had I not made that same investment in myself and shared with people that I understood how terrifying it was. From there, I easily doubled my income in 2010 to half a million.

When people become entrepreneurs and launch their own businesses, they have visions of how it's going to be, which is always different from their jobs. They want more freedom and flexibility, working with the clients they choose. The sky is the limit in terms of income, so they end up working all the time thinking the harder they work the more income they will make. I see moms starting their businesses because they want to spend more time with their kids, and they're not doing that. Their business takes over their lives.

I take a stand for my entrepreneurial lifestyle, starting with clarity in my marketing. There are not many people out there truly working part-time. They talk about it, but few are actually doing it. At first I needed time with my daughter. When she started school full-time, instead of working more, I chose to keep my part-time schedule and create "me" time. Maintaining this lifestyle takes a lot of saying no and letting go; saying no to non-ideal clients and joint ventures that won't attract my ideal clients. I work three to four days a week, and the people I attract desire a similar schedule.

When I decided that my ideal clients will want to invest in themselves at the level I've invested in myself *and* they want peaceful part-time prosperity, that's what I created. That takes getting clarity about the clients and activities most aligned with what you want to create and being able to hold that line.

I also attract many sales and marketing experts who are frustrated and embarrassed because they can't do it for themselves. That's because they're too close to it. In most cases they were selling copiers, pharmaceuticals, land or houses, but not their own gifts and talents. Many of my clients are frustrated because they don't know how to talk about what makes them great or even describe what they do. I tell them until they own how awesome they are, they won't be able to translate that into their marketing.

When I had that initial three-hour session with Lisa, she asked me some questions that I ask my own clients. At first it really made me mad but I realized I have my blind spots. That also speaks to being the client you want to attract. I want my clients to be humble enough to know when it's time to get help even in areas where they are supposed to be the expert. In that sense, I was the client I wanted to attract when I invested in mentorship from Lisa.

Grab your free gift from Lisa Cherney
at <u>www.MeetTheSassies.com</u> today.

Step Three
Make
Sassy Money

> "Box yourself in and sell a product or program that you haven't created yet. It's a surefire way to get yourself in action."
>
> —**Lisa Sasevich**

Chapter Seven
Build the Plane as You Fly It

There is a tendency as an entrepreneur marketing your business to overanalyze and make everything absolutely perfect—your website copy, your signature speech, the handouts you give to the audience at your talks, and on and on with every little detail. The reality is that even though we are all aiming for having the perfect brand and the perfect moment with our audience, the magic really happens by taking inspired action even though it is imperfect action.

Go for "Good Enough"—Take Imperfect Action

Sometimes you're scared, it's a big leap to get out there, to be vulnerable. Sometimes we're afraid of our own power, afraid of failure or afraid of success. Change is scary. Getting out there is scary. You can sit there and refine something until it's perfect but what's actually happening is that you're hiding, and that's a disservice to the people who need what you have to offer. Sure, the first time you speak you're going to make mistakes, you will stumble, but if you're speaking from your heart, with your passion and your expertise, no one will care—they'll be focused on the message and the transformation. The truth is your audience is rooting for you and really wants you to do great!

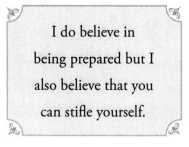

I do believe in being prepared but I also believe that you can stifle yourself.

Recently, I received a call from *More* magazine wanting to interview me. I was able to squeeze in a brief interview between two other calls. I had no time for research and I didn't even have the information in front of me that the writer wanted to ask me about. And yet I knew I was supposed to speak to that audience. So I did it, and it was imperfect and it was inspired. It was also a great connection for me, and a great interview.

The magic really happens by taking inspired action even though it's imperfect.

I do believe in being prepared but I also believe that you can stifle yourself with getting ready, and that sometimes, you can just go with "good enough," especially when it comes from an inspired thought. When that little voice inside you says, "You have to do this" or "Wow, look at that!" and you hear the other voice say, "No, that's too quick," or "No that's too expensive" or "No, you don't have the time," to me that's an indicator that you received genuine inspiration. And with an inspiration or a download, that other voice of resistance will always come up to question you. So when I hear that voice of resistance, I say, "Oh, perfect! Now I know I had an inspired thought," and off I go to take action. The important thing is to keep moving forward, and your automatic guidance system *will* kick in. Rest assured, you will get the guidance you need.

Build the Plane as You Fly It

Here's how to get your business to take off in a bold way, to stretch yourself by taking this concept of imperfect action a bit further. Once you've outlined your Unique Branded System, it's quite natural to fill it in with a whole bunch of content. But that's where the heart-centered entrepreneur can get a little bit stuck.

You are already an expert in what you do, and now you've mapped out your Unique Branded System, with three or five or seven steps. Even though you haven't filled in all the content for those steps, I urge you to do what I did—take your next step and sell a training series, or sell a mentorship, or a one-on-one coaching package. You have enough information just with the transformation you provide. The steps you've outlined to provide your expertise are enough right now to actually, believe it or not, put people into your coaching program, your mentorship, your course, your workshop—whatever you decide to do.

This is called building the plane as you fly it, this is boxing yourself in. If you sell somebody into

> Don't get too wrapped up in designing all of your content. Once you know the process, you can trust your blessing.

a course that doesn't exist yet, you will have it ready by the time the first class comes around, I promise you. You are a person of integrity and while you may push your own priorities back and back and back, when it comes to delivering your blessing to those who need and value it . . . you will! That's how I started with my business. I didn't have anything. I spoke from the stage. I created the idea of a book and called it *Designing and Presenting Irresistible Offers*. People bought it. I told them it was going to be ready in 90 days, and it was ready in 90 days. Now my company earns $5,000 to $10,000 a month in online sales at www.theinvisibleclose.com

with that product. I created it four years ago, and sold it when it didn't yet exist.

Don't get too wrapped up in designing all of your content. Once you know the process, you can trust your blessing. You know what needs to go under each of those steps. And three days before you're supposed to deliver that first course, you will fill in the blanks and you will get on that teleseminar, or on the phone with your one-on-one client, and you will lead an amazing session. It's *in you* already.

Make it real in the world and nothing will motivate you more and get your business moving faster! Certainly not sitting at your computer dotting i's and crossing t's and triple checking your sales copy. Selling a program or a product or a book that doesn't exist is the best way to make those products—and your business—"real."

How to Make Every Product a Best Seller

One of the biggest benefits of building the plane as you fly it is that you're able to make sure everything you're creating is truly in demand in your market. When you sit down and create something in its entirety and then launch it into the world, you're taking a big chance that what people need, want and desire is the same as what you *think* they need, want and desire.

But when you build the plane as you fly it, you make an offer for something you know you can deliver, but you haven't spent countless hours developing yet. And if the market is not interested, you don't need to go any further. If they *are* interested, you find out right away when people invest in it. You can pre-sell what is already developed inside you if you have confidence in your ability to deliver. This is how 100% of my product offerings have always been successful. I use all the tools that I share in this book, but I don't get ahead of myself guessing about what the market is demanding. If you use this system, you'll always be creating relevant products.

For example, if you have a free call on a topic and nobody shows up, it's probably not a path you want to be pursuing. But if you have a free call and hundreds or thousands of people opt-in or comment on your blog post, you know you're onto something hot, and you haven't invested thousands of dollars in a website, trademarking, logos—all the things people usually do before they've been able to establish that there truly is demand. If they don't bite, you make a few refunds and move onto the next product or service. This is a surefire way to test the market and never fail!

 Would you like to see our step-by-step "Build the Plane as You Fly It" process for creating your very first Training or Information Product? This is the key to being able to serve people all over the world with your knowledge and the first step to being able to make money while you sleep. You can access it now at www.Sassy21DayChallenge.com.

Zero to $100K in 17 Months

by
Nikkea Devida

When I joined Lisa's first Sassy Mastermind in October, 2009, I didn't even have a business of my own yet. I had taken a "hiatus" from my own coaching and training business as a subconscious belief change and Feng Shui expert to do corporate business consulting and training work with my husband. For those six years, I used my military and corporate project management, operations and systems background to help CEOs systemize and organize their businesses so they could accelerate their results and grow easily and profitably. I loved the challenge of the work, but I wasn't able to fully express all of myself, my expertise, or my gifts, which was leaving me very unfulfilled … despite my success.

I really struggled with how to re-create a successful and fulfilling business for myself doing what I loved with clients I loved. Because of my diverse background, I had several areas of expertise: subconscious belief change, Feng Shui, natural health and weight loss, producing live events, speaking from the stage, project management, professional organization, creating systems for anything, building teams and organizations, identifying ideal clients. Any one of them could have been a successful business. Lisa lovingly and jokingly refers to me as the "jack of all trades, master of all."

Fortunately, I realized that the Sassy group represented my ideal client—heart-centered entrepreneurs, messengers, and agents of change. I decided to offer free sessions to the Sassies in any area in exchange for a testimonial. I was shocked when they all picked the same thing—my subconscious belief change work. Happily armed with glowing testimonials and one area to focus on, I started creating and implementing my entire Leveraged Progression Plan based on the new mantra Lisa put in my head, "build the plane as you fly it."

I followed all of Lisa's teachings precisely. I created my signature talk, expert title, speaking package and my gifts page so I was ready and could say yes to any speaking engagement. Then I put up a landing page and sales page and conducted my first preview call to pre-sell my first online program using Lisa's 6-Figure Teleseminar Secrets.

When I did my first preview call, I had no online presence, no website, no e-zine, and no previous products. I took a cold list of prior clients (from email and business cards) who had not heard from me in six years, and 211 of them opted in to my call. Between the live call and the encore call, a total of 85 people listened. I named my very first signature talk "When Willpower, Affirmations And Positive Thinking Aren't Enough: 5 Simple Steps To Change Your Limiting Beliefs In Minutes ... Guaranteed." From the preview call, I pre-sold the 8-part teleseries called the "Accelerated Change Template (ACT) ™ Belief Change System" to 17 people.

Using Lisa's model, I presold the teleseries, which, when recorded, became my first information product called Accelerated Change Template (ACT) ™ Home Study Course and then my high-ticket program called the ACT Mentorship Program™. This was a huge leap of faith because I had been teaching subconscious belief change in a live workshop setting since 1997. Initially, I had a hard time figuring out how I was going to teach the visual components to my students and if it would work to teach it over the phone and in an online setting.

I solved the problem by hiring a video crew. We only filmed the sections that needed a visual compo-nent, and the rest I delivered through the teleseminar calls. This forced me to up-level my material to make sure it was very systemized and paint-by-number so my students would get a great result. I'd always been able to observe my students in my live workshops to ensure they were "getting it." With the virtual delivery, since I couldn't see them, the teaching modules had to go as smoothly as if I were right in front of them, watching over their shoulders. It went far better than I expected, and everyone loved it! Phew! The plane flew!

My other "build the plane as you fly it" experience in year one and year two of Sassy was to build my team, especially my virtual team, which was completely new to me. I hired a web person, a virtual assistant, a bookkeeper, a CPA, and a personal assistant. It took me several tries to assemble the right team, but I systemized the hiring, training, and managing process as I went and even created another information product called the "Accelerated Personal Assistant Program™." Systemizing this process for myself has now enabled me to free up over 40 hours per week to focus on the revenue generating activities in my business, plus get some sleep, and have a life! We even took our first real vacation in years and went to Italy.

The instruction, the guidance, the support, not only from Lisa, but from the other mastermind members as well, kept me on track. There were so many times when I got stuck along the way and didn't know how to do the next step, but there was always an answer within the mastermind so I could move forward. This focus kept me building the plane despite the turbulence and obstacles along the way. I simply focused on what to do next, and bit-by-bit, I built each part of my business.

When I became a Sassy, I was taking a stand to say "yes" to myself, my message…and most importantly, my music. I made a promise to myself (and the mastermind) that was nonnegotiable—whatever business I did, music had to be part of it. My ultimate joy, what feeds my soul, is music, singing and songwriting. Initially, I had no idea how that would manifest since I hadn't written, recorded or performed any music for over 14 years. But at the very first Sassy retreat I was inspired to write a theme song for Lisa. She caught the vision and hired me to make it real!

The lyrics just flowed and through a divine connection with another songwriter, we co-wrote Lisa a song called "Make Money With Your Thing." It was truly a peak life experience to perform it live at Lisa's Speak-to-Sell event in 2011, and I'm honored that it has now become Lisa's theme song!

I was also inspired to write a song as my personal tribute and as a tithe to raise money and awareness for female veterans called "Our Sisters Who Serve." As a disabled veteran myself, my goal is to raise $1 million for these too-often unsung heroines.

As a year three Sassy, my two big goals now are to have my own three-day event and to become Lisa's first $0 to 7-figure, 3 years to 7 figures success story. For me, that's just the next level of plane to build as I fly! And with Lisa's teachings and the Sassy Mastermind, I know it's possible. In fact, I've taken this teaching so much to heart that my new brand is called "The

Soaring Entrepreneur: Serve with Honor, Prosper with Pride, Fly to Freedom." This will also be the theme for each day of my first event.

By continuing to "build the plane as I fly it," I have a clear plan for my new business to generate $1 million dollars this year, which represents thousands of lives touched and transformed by my work, but I am also committed to raising $1 million for women veterans, which is why I'm having my first event right before Veteran's Day.

I've modeled and implemented each step of Lisa's curriculum fully in each year of the Sassy program, and the results have been amazing for me both personally and professionally—starting at zero and working my way up—way UP!

Grab your free gift from Nikkea Devida
at www.MeetTheSassies.com today.

Show Up, Sparkle and Be Heard

by
Kay White

Ialways knew I'd be writing a book and my guidance knew it too because as soon as I became a Sassy I started seeing the signs everywhere. Sassies help each other out and when I helped publisher Bob Burnham get unstuck with his Unique Branded System, as a thank you he gifted me with a copy of his book when I saw him next at Lisa's live event. During the event Lisa mentioned her book, I happened to sit next to her book editor and I also shared a room with someone whose husband was writing a book. All signs.

Flying home to England, I was watching a very efficient, friendly flight attendant connecting with people, looking after them, making them comfortable, offering them a drink. He was doing what needed to be done without being pushy. I thought, what is it that he is doing so naturally that so many people struggle with? I started reading Bob's book and thought about the message I had just received at Lisa's event, to get out there doing your "thing." I thought, I can do this with my eyes shut.

I picked up my journal and wrote:

"Here I am reading Bob's book *101 Reasons Why You Must Write A Book,* and I will."

As if being guided, I wrote A, B, C all the way to Z and filled in the 26 principles of what was to become *The A to Z of Being Understood.* Twenty-four of those 26 principles are in the book exactly as I penned them. I also decided it would be a number one bestseller before my birthday in June (only eight months away). And then . . . I did nothing.

My business, Way Forward Solutions, helps women (and very smart men) who struggle to connect and engage people become comfortable saying what needs to be said respectfully and assertively. This is very rare in business these days. People think business is a win or lose proposition or they need to "Get one over on someone," or they must "Tell it like it is." But that just makes others angry. I show people how to say what needs to be said without upsetting people, being disrespectful or burning bridges. With my own system, my 7-step LINKING Your Thinking™ formula, you can be yourself, say what needs to be said and get what you want. As I worked with more and more clients, they began to ask me where they could they read about it and learn more.

As a Sassy Mastermind Member at the Diamond level, I fly from my home in London to the USA to attend three retreats per year and receive business strategy sessions with Lisa. When I mentioned I was working on a book, Lisa cautioned me not to let the book stop me from doing everything else in my business. Some people take a year off to write their book, making little money and losing touch with their clients. Lisa suggested doing e-zine articles and turning them into a book.

Lisa gave us Sassies the book *The War of Art,* which she said would put distinction around something we all struggle with: resistance. The next morning, December 16th, in bed at 5:30, I read a few pages. Right away, the book completely irritated me because it was describing me. I was doing everything but sitting down to do the work, because I knew it would be hard and overtake my life. I set the book down and started writing.

I wrote "A is for Attitude," then joined the other Diamonds for breakfast. Sitting next to us were two U.S. Navy pilots. I knew "attitude" was an aviation term and I took this as another sign. I asked them what the word "attitude" meant to them and I received a line that's now in my book, "It's the angle your nose meets the wind." This is exactly what the first chapter of my book is about – how you approach something.

From there on, every morning I got up at 5:00 and I wrote until 6:30 until I finished on February 20th. Sassy Bob and I reverse engineered that date because I wanted to be on stage at Lisa's event in June with my best-selling book in my hand.

One of the opportunities of being a Diamond is getting exposure to Lisa's list. I immediately thought of my book. She said in that wonderfully light and breezy way fantastic ideas tumble out of her, "Why don't you make it a teleseries?" And said I could divide it into five parts, give five points from the book in the first preview call, with the opportunity to learn the rest in my offer. We did the email blast and 800 people signed up for the call, which grew my list substantially.

Seven people signed up for the teleseries, which more than covered putting the whole thing together. I recorded the teleseminar and then made a product.

It was truly a real build the plane as you fly It experience, because I was still writing the book as I was giving the teleseminar! It lit a fire under my seat, as I was only one week ahead of the teleseries. There was a lot of juggling to do, but my husband was so excited for me and he could really see the difference it was making in me and my business. The more I was talking about the book and what I was doing, the more people were interested and wanting to work with me. Articles from my e-zine that were already written became chapters in the book, so I was leveraging everything.

It was a real ride, writing, publishing and teaching the book all at the same time. The book became a number one bestseller within three weeks of being released. Truly exhilarating, and afterward I had a bit of a rough landing following the intensity of being lit from within by my purpose. It took me a good six weeks to be up and running again. But business is a marathon, not a sprint. I had sprinted for seven or eight months. A Sassy friend told me sprinters needs periods of rest, and marathoners must have huge periods of rest to regroup. I hadn't had any. In my exhaustion, I cried when she told me that because she gave me permission to feel the emptiness. "I don't know what to do next," I said. "That's the point—you don't have to do anything."

In building the plane, there comes a point when the plane is built and you need to just fly it. And fly it I did and still am. As a number one best-selling author, I've been offered so many speaking engagements and interviews, and my book is already being taught at a university within six months of being published. It still makes me catch my breath!

In my business, I've gone from having a very low-key, face-to-face, one-on-one executive coaching rather blah business to having a specialized niche with clients from all over the world. I now earn in six weeks what I used to earn in six months.

My signature program is called "Show Up, Sparkle, and Be Heard," and I'm passionate about helping women (and very smart men) get their point across, make connections and say what needs to be said, and really own their personal power to be themselves and to add a bit of sparkle to their conversations. By directing the attention to the other person, using their name and remaining engaged and present, they can say virtually anything because they've made them feel heard and powerful.

Those who learn my LINKING-your-Thinking ™ process become more promotable and get more business, are more confident and assertive, yet are still respectful. You can be a ball-breaker and still get things done, but people don't like you. With my system, people wonder why they are doing something for you, but the funny thing is, they really want to. There's a way to accomplishing that, and that's what I've been able to distinguish.

Being part of Lisa's group has made me crystal clear on my gift. I was meddling in what Lisa calls "my blessing" for years, but the essential "thing" I do is the same; I'm still saying, "Give me five minutes and I'll tell you how to be a savvy communicator." Now, though, I make a huge difference and a lot of money at the same time. That's what I call Sassy!

Grab your free gift from Kay White
at www.MeetTheSassies.com today.

"Aim, Fire, Ready"
to Turn Ideas into Reality

by
Bob Burnham

My dad was the type of guy who literally worked on a project for a year or two before he pulled the trigger. Often by the time his venture was unveiled, it didn't connect. Sure, that's what entrepreneurship is all about, but at the same time, if he had done it with Lisa's build the plane as you're flying It method, he could have saved years of struggle. I've learned so much from that concept.

When I first sold my DVD product, "Write & Publish Your Own Book in 40 Days: Simple Secrets to Making a Six Figure Income As an Author," I didn't even have it produced. The first time I called up continuing education to teach a course, I didn't have a course description written. Not only do I believe testing the waters first is not a negative thing to do, it's actually the best thing to do. When you start taking action, even though you might not be totally prepared, the universe has an absolutely magical way of coming in and supporting you. Even when you take imperfect action or wrong action, extraordinary things really do start to happen.

I help coaches, entrepreneurs, consultants and speakers write books to position them as experts so clients pursue them, rather than having to pursue clients, which is much more costly and time-consuming. Being pursued also attracts more ideal, higher-paying clients. From chapter titles that make readers want to buy, to promoting and building products and workshops from their books, I teach authors how to make money.

After building and selling a company that grossed $6 million per year, I wanted a more meaningful business, and Expert Author Publishing was born. Since 2005, I've worked with 240 authors, building their existing business with a book or making their book into a business itself.

The most lucrative advice I received from Lisa includes taking people from interested to invested in one phone call, and learning to leverage myself, because a lot of what I do with each client is the same. Leveraging has increased my profits substantially—I've run coaching programs from 5 to 25 people at a time. Lisa also made me realize prices are elastic, and the more I value the information I share with my authors, the more I can charge. Her advice on building a higher-ticket program is a game-changer for me. Plateauing at $15,000 a program, Lisa convinced me that having my own three-day event would bring me more committed, action-taking, higher-paying clients.

Since I've been in the Sassy Mastermind, my profits have increased by 400%. I get so blown away at some of the things that have happened in my business as a result of what I've learned from Lisa, but the whole idea of building the plane as you're flying it is pure genius.

One of my father's inventions was a dial-a-line copy holder. Back when typewriters were the norm and there were no scanners, if you were typing from another document, a dial would move a marker down so the next line of text to type could be clearly seen. I watched him work on this for a couple of years, filing for patents and getting the prototype together. If he had just gone out and sold the concept outright, he might have found a buyer, but two years later he discovered no one really wanted it. What if he had gone to office supply stores, told them the product would be available shortly and asked if they interested in purchasing it? If he got a negative response, he could have saved himself tens of thousands of dollars and a couple of years of work.

I didn't realize until I was in my teens how stressful it was doing it his way, because each project took so much time, energy and money before he got an answer, and our family was starting to feel the pinch. With Lisa's formula, you find out the answer almost right away. You can try several things in the time my dad took to try one thing, and be that much closer to a successful outcome. Let's face it, entrepreneurs have failures, or at least they should if they are trying a variety of things, so the quicker you get through the failures, the quicker you get to success. That's why building the plane as you fly it is such a sound principle.

Many of my clients really fight this idea. One client was asking me about a good price to build a website and price ranges for his packages. I told him he was going about it the hard way, putting all this time, effort and money into something he didn't know would work. He needed to get out there and start talking about his packages, he'd find out right away whether people wanted them or not. The other way is too risky.

I realized some people may feel like frauds offering a product that doesn't exist in order to gauge interest, but I don't believe that. There's nothing wrong with putting it out in the world to find out if there is value in it. If not, why waste the time? It's on to the next thing. Some clients say they'd feel they were lying, but if you look at it through different eyes, you'd actually end up creating better value for everyone because you get feedback—you find out people's likes and desires, what they're willing to pay for, and how much.

I sold four of my DVD sets the first time I offered them and told the audience I would ship them within 30 days. Then I had someone videotape my next lecture and that became my DVD product.

This principle has also helped me when I speak

with someone who has an idea for a book or product but says they're not ready yet. I truly believe that once you step up and say you're ready, you *are* ready. It always works, and you always get the answers you're seeking once you start on your path. Lisa really helped that idea hit home with me.

My dad worked on several inventions and products from the time I was 14 until he died when I was 28. He never had a hit. If he had used building the plane as you fly it, he could have asked better questions, received better answers, shortened the time for completing his inventions, and kept moving forward.

Grab your free gift from Bob Burnham
at www.MeetTheSassies.com today.

Network Like a Pro – How My Own Program Worked for Me!

by
Sue Clement

When I first started coaching, I would occasionally get booked as a Lunch and Learn speaker at large corporations. Since I'm somewhat of a procrastinator, I'd usually wait until the last minute to prepare for my talks. As a way to overcome procrastination, I'd invite a few friends over for a dress rehearsal to practice my speech in my dining room. This was a great way for me to get started.

I had always wanted to speak to larger audiences though, so when the opportunity came to present at a conference, I jumped on it. Although I had no idea what to talk about, I came up with a catchy title: The 5 Biggest Networking Mistakes. I wasn't sure what they were just yet, but I was certain I'd be able to figure it out.

Months went by and suddenly the conference was coming up. One day I had this brainwave that instead of a dress rehearsal in my dining room, I should rent a hotel boardroom and hold a free evening seminar—to up the ante a wee bit.

I talked it up in all my networking groups and bought Ticketmaster custom tickets printed with "Network Like A Pro." (The original name wouldn't fit on the tickets!) Everywhere I went, I handed the tickets out like candy, telling my networking buddies, "Give them to everyone you know."

And then the work began! I had to find a way to sign up the attendees so I'd know how many chairs to put in the room. That was my biggest nightmare. I was frantic about having too many chairs. I attended a seminar once where the speaker set the room for 100 chairs and only eight people showed up. If that happened to me, I would be mortified.

The registrations were overwhelmingly impressive and the numbers kept climbing. Initially, I thought 20 would be great, and suddenly we had 40, 60, 80! I called the hotel and booked a larger room. Later I called back and asked for the whole ballroom. They said it would hold 175, and at that point I had over 200 registrations, but of course not everyone would show up ...

It seemed like every time I had a new idea, it required building a new system. There were so many moving parts! For starters, I had to send out 200 individual reminder e-mails, and then there were more questions: Where would everyone park? How would I know who showed up? How to get contact info from new guests? What about walk-ins? We needed a registration form, and a way to check off names. Then I decided to have door prizes ...

I also had to figure out what to sell at the back of the room. I chose one of my programs called "Get Clients Now." Each day something new would come up. This little "dress rehearsal" was constantly expanding. It was like making bread, covering it, and finding this monstrous thing growing. Then you punch it down and it grows some more!

I finally came up with my "5 Biggest Mistakes," fleshed them out, created the flipcharts and wrote out the seminar the night before. I was definitely building the plane as I flew it, and it was fun, wild, overwhelming and exhausting.

The day of the event was crazy. I didn't have a Virtual Assistant at the time, so I had to do all the prep work myself. I enrolled two friends to man the registration table, another one at the product table, and positioned my husband as the doorman. I told him "Nobody goes in that room without giving you their green registration form!"

And what about those chairs? I was still in a panic about having just the right number, with no way of knowing what that number would be. I didn't want a ton of empty chairs, especially in the front row, so I made a guess and had the hotel set the room up for 140 with some extra chairs stacked in a back corner.

I was absolutely obsessed, more concerned about the chairs than my presentation. Finally my husband said, "Enough with the chairs already!"

As it turned out, we had to keep adding chairs because more and more people kept showing up. I ended up with 187 attendees for a 175 capacity room! What a rush!

During the presentation, I had two breaks where people were able to network and practice the skills I was teaching, and it was just phenomenal. After everyone left—they stayed forever—I couldn't wait to get my hands on the feedback forms. I had posed three questions and the overall rating was a 4.6 out of 5. The seminar was a hit! It was one of the most rewarding, exhausting, exciting moments of my life.

Speaking of rewarding—three people bought my offer, $1000 for a six-week program, and I increased my list substantially. My "Network Like a Pro" seminar turned out to be one of my best list-building tactics. I didn't do it with that in mind, but that was certainly one of the benefits. It was such a great success and it was so much fun, I ended up doing this seminar three or four times a year with many repeat participants attending. Suddenly I was in the seminar business!

As great as those seminars were for my business, I knew I wanted more. I joined the Sassy Mastermind as a recovering lone wolf—I'm a competitive, self-reliant, do-it-yourself person. That worked very well for me when I grew my first company from startup to $5 million. In fact, I built my business entirely through cold calling. But after I sold it and started coaching in 2000, I realized that cold calling didn't work for getting coaching clients, so I had to learn how to get clients through networking.

At first, networking was hard for me, but I worked at it and quickly became an expert, teaching others how to do it effectively. But I also wanted to leverage my expertise to reach a much wider audience.

Yet by 2010, I still hadn't achieved the success I wanted. I looked around and saw other successful people I admired all supporting each other, and realized that the key thing they had in common was a tribe, and I didn't. To get farther I needed to connect more, and, in essence, find my tribe.

I was really attracted to the Sassy Mastermind because I wanted to follow in Lisa's footsteps. I admire her and I too want to share my gift with hundreds of people. Other than my coach, I didn't really have any peers I worked with so joining a mastermind with nearly 100 amazing participants has been nothing short of an exceptional experience. The growth for me has been learning how collaborate with others.

I've come a long way from that first talk on networking. Now, I'm known as The Networking Pro in my area. As a sought-after speaker, I've been invited to present across the country and internationally as well! I've hosted dozens of teleseminars and webinars, and wrote a book called *Insider Secrets to Referral Success*. One of my favorite programs is my high-level Referral Success Bootcamp, where I help business owners put an end to their feast/famine cycle by developing referral relationships.

The funny thing is that I speak and coach others on what I needed myself, and that's why becoming a Sassy has been so important to me. I'm finally learning to be part of a tribe where we help each other with ideas, encouragement—and referrals!

Grab your free gift from Sue Clement
at www.MeetTheSassies.com today.

> "Tension is good, it's the internal force that motivates people to take action and better their lives."
>
> —**Lisa Sasevich**

Chapter Eight
Invite Pursuit

It's a Disservice Not to Make an Offer

This chapter is a little longer because, as you'll soon see, it's my favorite subject ... making irresistible offers!

Why should you make an irresistible offer to your prospective clients? From my perspective, it's a disservice *not* to. You see, when someone shows up to see you, they are giving you a message. Whether they show up for your live talk, or on the phone for your teleseminar, or you are asked to be a guest speaker on someone else's stage or telecall—even if someone speaks with you at a networking event where there are lots of different people they could engage with— they are giving you their time and attention. If they are reading your e-newsletter—one of the ways they can

217

discover you—they are also "opting in" to you. And what they are saying by giving you their attention is, "I have pain in the area of your expertise." Or "That's an area where I'm good, but I want to be better."

So even if they are saying "I'm pretty good," you can still translate that to "I have pain," because what they really mean is, "I have the pain of wanting to be great, even awesome—I know I have it in me and I want to reach my potential." There is some dissatisfaction there, there's a *gap* between where they are and where they want to be.

And when you think about it, if they're sitting there listening to you or engaging with you and there's not a gap, then why the heck are they there? Don't they have a few things they could be doing with their lives and with their time?

When I used to teach the understanding men workshops, I knew just by virtue of a woman coming to our free session, that by taking three hours out of her night and driving across a bridge in San Francisco after a busy day at work, she was saying, in essence, "This is an area where I need help." I didn't know if the help she needed was with her father, brother, son, boyfriend or husband, but I did know that she was looking to understand men better—it was very clear that she had a gap in that area.

> It's a disservice if you don't tell potential clients,
> "Here's how to get more from me."

If you've been doing what you're doing for 20 years and they spend an hour with you, how much transformation can you give? In most cases, the most we can do is get them to the place where the gap becomes apparent and they start asking themselves the serious question: "Am I ready to handle this? Am I ready to close the gap?"

So in order to succeed at getting more clients and helping more people, you need to shift your mindset from *trying to get sales* to *serving the people who have already shown by their initial interest they need what you have.* They may not be ready to transform it, they may not be ready to accept your offer, but they're there, and they're interested.

One of the clients I mentor works one-on-one with people as a spiritual healer. She started increasing her sales just by starting to make offers. She packaged up her irresistible offers for six sessions or six months, and started offering those packages before the client left after their first appointment. What a service this was for people! Otherwise what her clients had to do when they needed her help was go through the whole sale in their heads all over again. They were saying to themselves, "Is this problem big enough to call so-and-so and pay $150, $250 an hour, or should I muddle through it on my own?" But after a wonderful session where they commit to six more sessions, they don't have to "resell" themselves every time. They just figure, "I have pain in this area and she can solve it because I'm already booked for more sessions."

In this case, all my client did was package her services and just start making offers in her one-on-one practice, and if that's all you did after reading this book, it could make a huge difference. This client told me 75% of her clients enthusiastically invested in a package. She discovered she was taking care of her clients in an even better way by encouraging and offering possible options for them to continue their work with her.

Don't Tame the Tension: Tension vs. Pressure

As heart-centered entrepreneurs, pressuring people is what we all want to avoid. We don't want anyone to say they felt pressured and felt bad about their experience with us. So our tendency is to back off the whole way and not make an offer at all. This doesn't work either because it's a disservice to those who need you, and you get no sales.

Pressure is something that's applied *from the outside*. Tension is something that happens *inside of your potential clients.*

The key is to set the environment for them to feel tension, and there is internal tension when there's a gap between where they are and where they want to be.

Soon I'll cover some key elements for designing

truly irresistible offers that take that tension and move people into action, but first, I must answer a question I get asked quite a bit:

"Why do I need to make a special offer if my product is great on its own?"

Even if you have a fantastic product or service, which I'm assuming you do, you need to have a reason for your prospects to buy *today*, while they are inspired. To them, it must feel as if they would be missing out on so much if they waited that they will choose to buy today, rather than lose the deal.

People who take time to "think about it," rarely go back—even if they are super inspired in the moment. The times I have left to "go think about it," I simply went back to my life, where the priorities of being a mother and businesswoman became more immediate than registering for something that later just seems like it will be too hard to fit in.

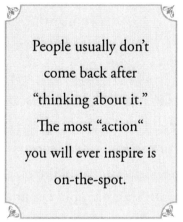

People usually don't come back after "thinking about it." The most "action" you will ever inspire is on-the-spot.

This is a crucial point: People usually don't come back after "thinking about it." The most "action" you will ever receive is on the spot.

Boost Sales Using Irresistible Offers

How do you get people from interested to invested, to liking what they hear from you to buying what you have? Have these scenarios happened to you?

People tell you: "You are so amazing, someday I'm going to work with you," but someday never comes.

"I love your work, I can't believe everybody doesn't know about you. You're the best-kept secret in your field." The first time you hear that it's a compliment, but after you've heard it for a while, it's just takes the wind out of your sails.

It's frustrating to be the best-kept secret in your field or to have a vibrant connection with clients but fall short of making the sale. Most heart-centered entrepreneurs are concerned about being pushy or salesy, so they fail to make an offer at all. This creates a self-fulfilling prophecy that keeps you the best-kept secret. The best way to make an offer without being pushy or salesy is to inspire action with an irresistible offer.

Let me give you an example of what I mean by increasing sales using an irresistible offer:

My client was hosting a series of evening events, where mostly women attended to learn about cosmetic laser treatments and receive a free laser hair removal treatment. These were upscale evenings with appetizers and assorted beverages, and every guest received valuable education whether they bought anything or not.

I was hired to make these events more profitable. At the event, I was happy to find an impressive turnout, and a presentation that was well-delivered and packed with information. Nothing to correct there! But when they got to the end of the presentation, the problem became obvious. There was no "Tonight Only Irresistible Offer."

The company did offer a couple of discounts and a few package deals, but never presented these as "tonight only." No pen or registration form was put in people's hands, they simply listed their offerings and left it at that. This is very common.

You see, because this crowd consisted of affluent clientele with some celebrities on the guest list, the owner was very wary of appearing pushy or salesy. Like most of us who own our own businesses, he didn't want people to feel like they were being "closed" or pressured in any way.

Now I agree that making people feel pressured is not the way to sell, in fact, it will hurt your reputation. The problem is that oversensitivity to

> With an irresistible offer, the owner does not have to apply pressure to his prospects, they apply it to themselves.

appearing salesy leads to overcompensating by rendering no offer at all, and the end result is a lot of lost sales and missed opportunities.

The key to having people feel compelled to register for your programs without feeling pressured has to do with how you structure your special offers. In the case of this cosmetic laser business, I went in and restructured their offer so the client would get a significant discount and some great free services if they purchased one of the three special packages within a week. And clients who purchased their package the night of the event received significantly more free bonus services.

This was a perfect solution because the owner did not have to apply pressure to his prospects. The guests applied it to themselves as they attempted to figure out whether it was worth it to leave hundreds of dollars of valuable services behind in exchange for a week to think about it. In most cases, if they were interested, they did the "sales job" on themselves, and this allowed the owner to remain calm and easygoing. He could assume the attitude that: "These are great specials. You are welcome to take up to a week to decide which is best for you. If you are ready to go and would like to invest tonight, you will also get the additional savings and bonus services we are offering tonight only."

For the duration of the event, the owner remained relaxed and of service, helping attendees figure out which package was right for them so they could

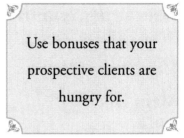

Use bonuses that your prospective clients are hungry for.

make a purchase that night and enjoy the best deal.

The conversion results at these events went through the roof by offering this no-pressure irresistible offer, averaging a 60% close rate for packages costing a few thousand dollars each. Needless to say, the owner was extremely pleased.

Use Limiters to Inspire Action

One of the biggest mistakes that rookies make when they are first getting out there to make an offer is that they forget to put a limiter on it. The limiter is what makes the offer irresistible—it's "today only" or it's "only for the first X number of people." When I'm on a live stage, I use both of those. I have a special price or special package for "today only." Once I walk out the door, it's gone. Then I usually have something extra just for the first X number of people to get them really popping out of their seats and to acknowledge the action takers, the people who are decisive and eager to invest in themselves. They know it in their gut and they are ready to go. The limiters help them follow their knowing and get into action.

Structuring Your Irresistible Offer

There are two parts to an Irresistible Offer—Your Main Dish and Bonuses.

Main Dish

Most of you have a main dish offer. It's the main way you deliver the unique transformation you provide, via your Unique Branded System, a five step this or that. It's your main course. If you look at a restaurant menu, there are appetizers, desserts and the main dish. So it's good to take inventory and look at what main dishes you have. For example, *The Invisible Close* is a main dish system that teaches you how to use irresistible offers to make more sales without being pushy or salesy—and it comes with bonuses.

Bonuses

If the main dish is a steak, bonuses are more like dessert. They may be an additional training session, a one-on-one call or it may be a call you did that you recorded and now you're offering as a bonus—and it's already made. It's nice to find things that you have already created to offer as a bonus. An easy one is obviously time with you. So you want to do a little inventory of all the things you can think of that could be bonuses. The key is to package your knowledge or service so it provides a high perceived value but costs you very little to deliver.

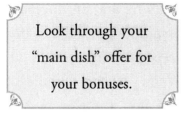

Look through your "main dish" offer for your bonuses.

Here's the million-dollar tip. Say you're creating a package and trying to make a bonus and you can't find anything, or you don't have the time to create something new. Instead of getting wrapped up in a whole new project of creating a bonus, look in your main dish offering and find something that is already in there that is really hooky and really cool and pull it out and make that the bonus.

For example, when I was first crafting *The Invisible Close*, I knew a big hook for people was that they wanted the sample order forms I use to present irresistible offers. So rather than hide them in the main dish where they wouldn't be appreciated, I took them out and made them a bonus. You get a CD with the Power Points on it of my sample order forms so you don't have to go get your forms made by a designer. You can just use my order forms and put your offer on them. So it's a bonus item. Voila! Everyone wins!

What I like to see with bonuses is that they are relevant and related. So if you're going to have one product like *The Invisible*

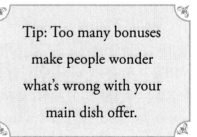

Tip: Too many bonuses make people wonder what's wrong with your main dish offer.

Close, you might have two bonuses. And you think:

what would someone who is buying that product naturally want? In our case it was sample Irresistible Offer forms to model, and an audio of me explaining it all. Keep it simple and relevant. When you add a whole lot of bonuses that aren't tightly related, it makes people think: What's wrong with the main dish?

Little Soldiers

A little soldier is a bonus that you gift to your buyers. They benefit you and your buyers by giving them a way to share what they just bought with a friend, another potential client for you.

An example would be when we added a CD of our introductory presentation from the understanding men course as a bonus for women who bought that night. Obviously, if a woman signed up for the workshop, she's already sat in the audience listening to this, so what is she going to do with that CD? She's going to pass it on to a friend. That's why I call it a little soldier—it's like your little troops out there marching for you, selling your stuff when you're not around.

Then we came up with one called "the gift for your girlfriend." So if you register today, you get extra bonuses, and one of them was a gift for your friend—$100 off if your friend came to the same workshop you did. All the friend had to do was call and say, "I have a $100 gift and I want to register for the same workshop as Sally." We did no additional marketing and filled one more workshop seat. Little soldiers are feet on the street drumming up sales for you even when you're not there!

Be Committed But Not Attached

Committed but not attached is a mindset, an attitude and place to come from to close sales more successfully without being salesy. What you're committed to is that your potential clients make a decision. I don't want my prospects to leave with one more thing to think about or figure out. I do everything I can to support them to make a decision on the spot and move forward.

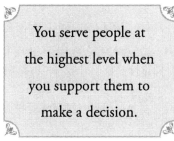

You serve people at the highest level when you support them to make a decision.

But here is the key: I'm not attached to what their decision is. Yes or no is fine. It's the "maybe" that's the deathblow to their transformation and adds an unneeded piece of clutter to their lives.

Nobody needs one more to-do on their to-do list, such as going to check a website, doing additional research about your program, or, worst of all, taking time to "think about it." Do they ever do that, really? Realistically, it's ridiculous that someone would need to go check your website when you, the creator of all of it, is standing right in front of them. Making a decision on the spot not only empowers your potential clients, but supporting them to make that decision will empower you.

> Someone being pursued cannot pursue—there's just no space for it.

Being committed but not attached allows you to invite pursuit rather than being a pursuer. I learned from Alison Armstrong, an early mentor, that pursuit is a masculine characteristic. Just like the male anatomy, it protrudes and fills all the space. When you are pursuing someone, they have only two options: to submit, in which case you usually end up with a refund, or they can resist, which can turn off a potential client forever. In order for them to have the option to pursue you or your work, you have to make an invitation and leave enough space to allow them to step forward. Someone being pursued cannot pursue—there's just no space for it.

Irresistible offers invite pursuit and leave room for your clients to move forward and follow their desires to grow, learn and excel. Using your irresistible offers and being committed but not attached allows you to remain the trusted advisor who is there to bless them with your expertise should they decide to pursue an opportunity with you.

The Danger of Pursuit

by
Kiva Leatherman

I worked in the financial services industry and did extremely well quickly at a young age selling somebody else's words, thoughts and ideas. When I think back on that time, I see myself as a walking talking parrot. My job consisted of schmoozing. I repeated what I was taught or told by portfolio managers or marketing experts at huge $100-million-a year companies.

I thought I was really good at sales because I closed lucrative deals and made a lot of money. At that time in my life, those two things meant success to me. After making the leap into entrepreneurship, I didn't think sales would be a problem. I had that part down, I just needed to know my community and figure out my products and services, and go be a great salesperson again. Lo and behold, that's not what happened . . .

The dynamic is different when you're simply presenting what you have been told versus presenting your own ideas, your own philosophy, and your own beliefs. I remember the first time I did that in a networking meeting. I've done public speaking throughout my career and loved it (once speaking to a room of

1200 people). I was never scared. But when I started my business, I went to a local networking group and I had to stand up and introduce myself and describe my business. There were 50 people in the room and I felt nauseated. I was shaking and I sounded like a 10-year old. I could barely be heard across the room.

It wasn't until I realized that all I needed to do was be myself and speak my truth and people would resonate with me and come forward. Only then did I start to create revenue. But it took a few years of beating my head against the wall because I thought I still had to be salesy.

My business started after I crashed and burned out of my investment career. I had these two young babies and I was very depressed. I knew I could do more with my education and knowledge—I was wasting them and felt I had ruined my career. One day I was sitting on the couch pondering my options. I didn't want to go back to a regular job because the children were so little, but I needed to do something. There was a quote I had heard by Barack Obama in his inauguration speech about the creativity of men and women and how that could change the world, and all of a sudden I had this idea. I could teach women about money and finance from a feminine perspective, not in terms of the environment I'd just left, full of competition and all about high returns, but to teach them about worth from a practical standpoint, feeling worthy in every way. I had no idea what it would be like, except for the word "wise."

The result was Wise Women Network. I realized if I didn't teach women to find the core of their self worth, it wouldn't matter what I taught them about stocks, bonds and investing. Now I help women live their healthiest lives in all areas. My team and I present online programs called Wise Workshops so women can take back power in their lives, whether that's with money or parenting. Parenting is where I saw many women beat themselves up. It can be this eternal cycle of judging ourselves as not being good enough, either at home or at work.

Once I truly grasped the complexity of "women's worth" and Lisa's *Invisible Close* sales strategies when I joined the Sassy Mastermind, everything about my sales changed. Whenever you have a business that is idea-based or mission-based, the last thing you want from a client (or in one of your groups) is someone who isn't fully on board, someone who is "sold into a program." Ultimately you want people who are happy to be there and inspired to take this work out into the world in a huge way. This is especially true now that I'm creating parenting groups and a parent coaching certification program. It would be a huge disservice to my community, to my clients, to the other women participating to choose a sale over the integrity of the group.

When I get into an enrollment conversation now, I never pursue. It's about connecting with the person on a deep level and learning their point of view, their goals and dreams, what they want to achieve, their own sense of worth and how they feel about themselves, then making an offer if there's a fit. I invite them to join us with our mission and I truly take Lisa's advice that there is no attachment to that decision. Coming to that decision in that moment is the only thing that's important, so with their "yes" or "no," I let them know either way, it's a clean move onto the next thing. I've definitely had my, "Oh my gosh, if I don't get this client, I fail" moments. But that neediness, desperation and anxiety were skunk spray to potential clients.

Women especially want to make it easy for people, "Oh sure, take your time. Talk to your husband. Just get back to me whenever you can." Then there's still an energetic tie to that person and a nagging sense of "I should follow up" or "I haven't heard back from them." I would rather just hear the "no" and move on. If they say "no," they too can move on to their next thing and not be in a state of ambivalence or ambiguity.

My official contact list for Wise Women Network is slightly under 4,000 women now, and we've just entered into a strategic partnership with a list of 45,000. My radio show "A Woman's Worth" on Contact Talk Radio reaches 20,000 subscribers every week. I've had consistent 5-figure revenue for the last three months, and this year should be my first 6-figure year. There is no way I would be where I am today without the Sassy program, without Lisa's step-by-step formulas, and the support of the other Sassies. Without investing in mentors early on, I'd have a small local business. Now I have a platform that literally reaches around the world.

Grab your free gift from Kiva Leatherman at www.MeetTheSassies.com today.

My $42,000 Day
at the Office

by
Maribel Jimenez

Before becoming an entrepreneur, a lot of what I did was "business by the book," going to school, following the rules and doing everything "right." Being totally in my head was second nature to me; I had to control every part of my life. Since becoming an entrepreneur, I've had to throw that out the window. Tapping into my heart was where the real connection, the real passion, the real juice of my business was.

It has been a process of shifting and tapping into Source for me to go inside and find the answers. Finding a mentor like Lisa who runs her life by tapping in and being guided was a dream come true for me. She was exactly what I was looking for. I had many shifts and huge transformations right away once I learned to "go" before I felt ready and trust that I was supported. She is so willing to do it and model it that it gives me permission to do it myself.

I have three different brands around my business. My core business is Creative Solutions Consulting where I work with entrepreneurs and teach them how to market their message online. My second brand is Bake Your Book, supporting people further in getting their message out there in a big way through a book. My third brand is my newest brand, The New Superwoman Community, about sharing my personal journey with women so they can transform from the Superwoman Syndrome to the New Superwoman Syndrome, which is about living your life on your own terms.

The idea for The New Superwoman was divinely guided and it embodies all the work I've done in my life. I couldn't say no to that download!

Following Lisa's formula and philosophy has been really powerful. Lisa talks about being committed but not attached, and that is truly what's happening, not only in my sales conversations, but also in my business and in my life. I'm trusting that God has a better plan for me than I could ever have, so I'm committed to setting these goals and taking the action steps, but I'm not attached to how this might show up in my life.

Strategy sessions with clients are so different now because I'm trusting in Source that if this person is meant to become my client, that will be the natural next step, but I'm not attached. I'm simply committed to providing the best service I can. It's actually become pretty fun because amazing things are happening. I don't even try to plan it now, I trust that it will happen way better than I could imagine.

Before, I was trying to figure it all out and be steps ahead, going into a strategy session just hoping the person would say yes. In my heart I was so fearful that I went straight to my head. And my head was focused on trying to ask the right questions. But now that I'm tapped into my heart, I know the right things will be said.

My first speaking engagement was on a large stage in Canada, where I was giving an offer from the stage for the first time. I was scared to death. I almost talked myself out of it. Lisa teaches that your next growth area is the one that makes your knees buckle. I used visualization tools to see a big win for me: a powerful talk and a standing ovation. All sorts of resistance happened that could have completely thrown me off if I had been in my head; my PowerPoint disappeared off my laptop, I forgot my shoes . . . but I just let it go. I tapped into my heart and set the intention that what the audience needed to hear they would hear. Sure enough, it was an amazing experience and I *did* get a standing ovation. I had a line of women waiting to talk to me as soon as I was done, and e-mails and comments afterwards about the impact it had on people. I was on a natural high for a month.

At the Sassy Mastermind retreats, Lisa gives out

awards to acknowledge different areas of our growth, and I was onstage for all but one. As an entrepreneur doing things alone you don't often take time to acknowledge yourself, you just keep going. So that felt great. I was recognized for having the highest sale in one strategy session, signing up a client for $42,000. At the time, I wasn't hoping this client would say yes and planning out what I was going to say, trying to convince him to move forward, because by now Lisa's strategies had become second nature. I tapped into my heart, was guided by my desire to serve, and was clear that this call was really about how I could best serve this person. I was not attached whatsoever to the outcome.

Sure enough, he said yes. It was a great feeling to have the freedom of knowing that if he was meant to be my client it would work out, and that if he wasn't, he could say no and I didn't have to worry about that part because I did my part coming from service. I was willing to serve on a high level, which feeds my own soul.

I also received a Sassy Milestone Award for list building; mine grew from 2000 to 6200. Another award was for earning over 5-figures in one month!

My first exposure to Lisa was the 6-Figure Teleseminar series. At the time I was frustrated with putting so much effort into my first launch and getting flat results. At that point I wanted at least 1-figure teleseminar! After her series, I was able to have a

5-figure teleseminar. Lisa is such an excellent teacher. From there I continued to improve it and I'm sure this year I will have my first 6-figure teleseminar. I'm getting close and every launch has improved.

From that exposure, I knew my next big leap was going to be a high-level mastermind, so I joined Sassy just ready and willing to stretch however I needed to stretch to make things happen. I was prepared to have a quantum leap in my business. I was very selective about mentors. I wanted a mentor I could relate to on many levels, not just on business. I wanted a woman, a mother, and someone accomplished in all the areas in which I desired to have success. That was my intention, and Lisa was so willing to guide me to expand and be comfortable with being uncomfortable.

After joining Sassy, my first time making 5-figures a month happened quickly. Within that same month, I got my largest contract. Being willing to invest in myself and join the Sassy Mastermind shifted my energy because I was saying, "I'm worthy and I'm willing to make it happen." Sure enough it continued to happen and my business has at least tripled, if not more. This year it will at least double again. I am overjoyed and grateful to have Lisa and the other Sassies to support me in making quantum leaps.

Grab your free gift from Maribel Jimenez
at www.MeetTheSassies.com today.

Chapter Nine

Open the Road to Transformation

What is the Road to Transformation?

For the heart-centered messenger, the road to transformation is similar to a highway. Your ideal clients can access the highway from different on-ramps, depending on where they are in their awareness, their desire, and their willingness to invest in themselves.

When we look at your own unique offer and the unique outcome or transformation that you provide for your clients, the road to transformation is your personal "Transformation Highway" where your clients can come on and off at different points.

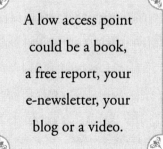

> A low access point could be a book, a free report, your e-newsletter, your blog or a video.

On the diagram on page 242, the bottom of the road to transformation is the "low" area. Here clients enter the highway from an on-ramp with a low investment. They have low intimacy and access as far as how much they work one-on-one directly with you.

Commitment
Action
Results

The Road to Transformation

Investment
Intimacy
Access

When you started your business, you probably worked one-on-one with clients. But as you leverage and organize your knowledge (as we showed you how to do in Chapter Three with the D.A.N.C.E. System), direct access to you, where clients come to your office for live, private sessions, becomes less necessary because clients can access your products and programs in other ways. High-ticket VIP days or VIP half-days where the client has your undivided attention and an opportunity for rapid transformation become your one-on-one options. This is further up the Transformation Highway.

Low access would mean your expertise would be delivered through a book, a free report, your e-news-letter, your blog or a video, and high access would include things like an interactive session with you.

As your clients come on to your Transformation Highway, the higher up they enter corresponds with them making a higher investment, with higher inti-macy and higher access to working directly with you.

The higher the investment, access and intimacy, the higher a client's commitment level to their success. As a result, they take more action. As the chapter quote says, people value what they pay for and they pay for what they value. This is good news for them and good news for you.

When clients are more committed and they are taking more action, they end up getting better results, and this creates a beautiful upward spiral for your business, because when you have clients who are committed and getting results, the good word about your business spreads, and as demand builds, you'll be able to charge higher and higher rates. So this is quite a beneficial upward spiral, and it's the sweet spot in your business. In summary, it leads to the following equation:

INVESTMENT + ACTION = RESULTS

And this is what we are all looking for with our clients!

Leveraged Progression Plan vs. Traditional Funnel

The Transformation Highway is part of your Leveraged Progression Plan. It is a bit different from the traditional marketing funnel where people enter at a free or very low ticket offer and then work their way up through a series of offerings until they get to your high-ticket service. The beauty of the Leveraged Progression Plan is it really allows you to "meet your client where they are."

Keep in mind that at any time potential clients can pull off the road at a service station to have a strategy session with you to up-level into a higher investment program. In line with the traditional funnel method, you will have clients who come in at low intimacy, low investment, low access programs to get started and get to know you, and you can always use a one-on-one sales model (ours is called ACTION Sales Secrets) to enroll them into a higher-end program.

If we examine the traditional funnel, for example, a client could download a free report from me, then invest in my $197 *Invisible Close* System, then attend a $997 Speak-to-Sell Event or join a 6-Figure Teleseminar Secrets virtual program, then they would be able to consider one of our high-end programs such as our Sales, Authenticity and Success Mastermind that requires a five-figure investment.

> The benefit of the road to transformation is that you can start serving highly committed, highly invested clients right away.

But with the road to transformation, the beauty is that someone can hear you speak free either on the Internet, in a teleclass or on a live stage, and there is a path for them to jump straight into one of your higher-ticket offerings if they are ready for that level of investment and action.

I've had clients who have never heard my name before who ended up hearing me speak on a 90-minute online presentation or as a guest on someone else's stage. Then they found their way to one of my live events and registered for a $100,000 Diamond Mastermind coaching program with me.

While there are certain places that overlap the traditional funnel, the benefit of this method is that you can start serving highly committed, highly invested clients right away.

Two Ways to Package and Offer Your Unique Branded System

Earlier in the book we talked about your Unique Branded System—the step-by-step process your clients use to gain the transformation you provide. The question is: Now that you have seen what the steps are, how do you package those so you can offer them at different price points on your Transformation Highway? There are two main ways to package your expertise.

1. The "One Core Program" Model

The first way to package your programs we call the "One Core Program" model. This is for you if you see that you have one core program, blueprint or step-by-step process that can be adapted to all the pricing and packaging options available. It is the same program, but the investment in the program increases with the level of intimacy and access the person would receive from you.

An example would be my Speak-to-Sell Bootcamp. This attracts people who want to use speaking to attract new clients and have them say "yes" on the spot. They gain the confidence that comes with being ready when they are invited to speak. There are a lot of ways for people to get their hands on that material, and which way they choose is dictated by the level of investment, intimacy and access they want.

Using my business as an example, my low invest-ment, low access, low intimacy product is my Invisible Close Sales Nugget E-Zine (actually it's no investment – it's free.) They have access to a ton of tips on Speaking to Sell every week, and what we find is that people who go no further than this level are less likely to take a lot of action, thus they tend to see fewer results. (Of course there are exceptions.)

Meanwhile, someone who wants to get their hands my whole Speak-to-Sell Formula in a more organized fashion can register for one of our live Speak-to-Sell Bootcamps. This has been offered during one of our early bird specials for as little as $997. At this live event, they make connections with hundreds of other like-minded entrepreneurs and receive all the training they need to craft their signature talk.

> With "The One Core" program, the program remains the same, but the investment, intimacy and access keeps increasing.

All year long we have people contacting us who need the Speak-to-Sell Formula right away. Suddenly they've got a speaking gig and they need all the DVDs and CDs from the workshop to study right in their living room. For this, they can go online and purchase the exact same training as the live event for about $1,997. Low intimacy, but the access to the material is right in their living room.

A few times a year I've been known to offer small group mentorships where I literally hold people's hands and walk them through the Speak-to-Sell Bootcamp in teleclasses. These consist of a very small number of people, so there's a very high level of access and intimacy to me. I become very familiar with their programs and I can support them with focused attention and personalized mentorship. These bootcamps have been offered for $7,500. Higher access, higher investment, same program.

Then we have the client who really wants my individualized attention. They want to come to my office and work with me one-on-one for half a day to put their talk together. We will be going through the exact same process they could have gotten for $997 if they went to the Speak-to-Sell Bootcamp live event, but because the level of intimacy is so high it is $13,000 at the time of this writing.

Corporations have sent their staffs to us for Speak-to-Sell training so the employees can be more effective in their speaking presentations. We have earned $50,000+ to train a group of team members from the same company with this exact same formula.

So you have essentially one program and the investment keeps increasing. You are simply saying to your potential clients, "Here is the transformation I offer. Would you like the carpool or the private limo?"

2. The Problem-Solution/ Problem-Solution Model

The other option is the Problem-Solution/Problem-Solution model. This is where you take your Unique Branded System and create a progression of products or services that offer a solution, and that solution reveals another problem. Say you came to me because

I can solve a particular problem for you. In this example, the problem would be you want to get known and make money. The solution would be for you get started speaking to build your platform and create your irresistible offers.

At the end of the program we point out that we delivered everything we promised but there's still a problem. If you are going to get out there, you need your signature talk. So the solution would be our next level of product offering, which is our Speak-to-Sell work.

We deliver all of that and make sure you are really happy with what you receive. Then the next problem you ask for advice about is: "How do I stop reinventing the wheel and actually build a business around my expertise?" So the next level is coming out for a special VIP day or joining my mastermind group.

You can take that system—it might be five steps—and each one of those could be leading to the next higher level of work that you do.

Get Discovered

When we look at the road to transformation and the packages you are offering at different price points, the next obvious question is: "How do people find out about me?" We use a hybrid model of both online and off-line marketing strategies (virtual and live strategies), and we break it down in a simple way since there are so many choices to get the word out about what you do.

There are four main ways for your ideal clients to discover you. For people who work with us in the year-long program, this is really what we focus on in the first year—how to build ways to be discovered, as well as building your programs. The reason we call this a Leveraged Progression Plan is because it's a plan for how a client progresses through your work, and it is leveraged because we are teaching you how to serve people beyond the one-on-one model, to serve multiple clients at the same time. Within the Leveraged Progression Plan there are four ways to get discovered:

1. Number one is online. In our model, we get known through our e-zine, or as a result of reading our blog, or via social media.

2. The second way to get discovered is through live networking or by referral. These are one-on-one types of situations that tend to occur in face-to-face meetings. This is where people are meeting you in person or on the phone.

3. The third is through what we call a preview call. This is on the telephone or through a webinar. You are either a guest speaking to someone else's followers, or you have a telecall or webinar with your own subscribers or followers.

This is also known as speaking virtually.

4. The fourth model is live speaking, where you're getting on a stage. Generally you are invited as a guest or as a featured presenter on someone else's stage so you can provide great content and also walk away with new clients.

One of the important things to know when you're exploring these models— and this is how I built a successful business in a couple of short years—is that with the online, live networking, and preview call models, you can generally be effective with converting clients up to a $1997 sale. If you've ever viewed any online

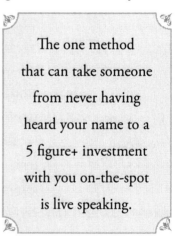

The one method that can take someone from never having heard your name to a 5 figure+ investment with you on-the-spot is live speaking.

marketing launches, they are generally selling products up to $1997 at the high end. The same price holds for any kind of webinar or preview call.

Of all four models, the one discovery method that can take someone from never having heard your name to a 5 figure+ investment with you on-the-spot is live speaking. Because of the credibility you gain from speaking on stage, the level of connection and intimacy you are able to create quickly because it's live, combined with your irresistible offers (which we explored earlier in this book), it's a formula that gives people everything they need to say "yes" to you on the spot.

Design Your Business Around Your Life!

When you're building your Transformation Highway it's important to remember the number one reason you became an entrepreneur and keep it at the forefront of your mind—your desire for a lifestyle that fits *you*.

Are you designing a life that you love?

We want to make a difference, we want to make big money and we want to enjoy the life we are living while delivering our work into the world. So I'm giving you the litmus test—four questions to ask yourself when you are crafting your irresist-ible offers and placing them on your road to transfor-mation. These questions will help you stay true to your own North Star and design a life that you love:

1. **What is the transformation I offer?** The first thing to do is get clear on the outcome or trans-formation you want for your clients.

2. **How will I deliver that?** What are the steps you take to deliver that with your Unique Branded System? And how will you deliver it? This means service delivery—will it be live work-shops, teleseminars or a book?

3. **Can it be leveraged?** Can you serve more than one client at a time or are you limited by the number of hours in a day to coach or mentor?

And the most important question of all:

4. **Do I love it?** You want to look back through your plan and make sure that you love what you have designed. Far too many people go through college, get married, get a job, design this entire life only to get it all and realize they don't love their daily lives. So I recommend keeping the phrase "Do I love it?" as your North Star right from the beginning.

In addition to what I've shared with you here, I've prepared a bonus training for you on something exciting I call "The Upward Spiral Effect." This is the key to having a business where you are paid handsomely and attract clients

 *who are highly committed, take massive action from your advice and get great results. Ahh ... Business nirvana! You can access this bonus training now at www.Sassy21DayChallenge.com.*

Monetizing
My Divine Mission

by
Amethyst Wyldfyre

The month before I started following Lisa's work, I made a total of $400 as a healer and psychic reader. From one piece of information she gave at her very first live event, I was able to start putting people on a list and making offers. I'd been taught by another mentor to give my products away, so for a year I gave away calls, reports, books, e-mail series, and I couldn't understand why nobody was buying. Lisa helped me see I needed a specific offer to invite people to go deeper. That one piece of advice turned my entire business around.

I had poured over half a million dollars into my business and personal growth work, racking up every credit card I had. By 2009, it was either succeed or get a job. I was a single mom and did not have the luxury of creating a $97 product and connecting with 100,000 people. Then I joined the Sassy Mastermind and created my first teleseminar series the next month, "Energize To Monetize," and priced it at $497. Eight people joined that series, and for the first time ever, I made money. I went from $400 in May to $4000 in June of 2009.

Soon after joining the Sassy Mastermind, I made my first $1997 offer. Three weeks later I spoke at an event for the first time and made an offer of $3997. Four people bought, which covered my investment in the mastermind.

I knew at the core of my being that my purpose was to serve in a very big way, globally helping messengers feel safe and powerful and able to prepare themselves to be heard by millions. I help them shift internally, and Lisa's work allowed me to connect with those I'm here to serve.

Once I started making real money, I was able to replicate those systems and make more money. I ran another program called Speaking Right Up, helping people clear their throat centers so they could speak their truth. When I joined the Sassy Mastermind, it was a huge eye-opener to see Sassies willing to invest at a high level in their businesses, with Lisa courageous and confident enough about her own blessings to be able to make that kind of offer. Lisa became someone to model for the courage and confidence to believe in herself and deliver results to justify that kind of offer.

I'm the poster child for anyone in healing work. Healers are so passionately desiring to serve. One of the biggest challenges we healers have is that we give give, give, give to the point of exhaustion, forgetting to take care of ourselves until we hit a dead end. There are so many amazing healers out there and their biggest challenge is valuing themselves appropriately, setting boundaries, and filling their own well. They can't make a global impact unless they have a healthy bank account.

Everything I have created is based upon my Unique Branded "Empower" system. Speaking virtually over the phone and Internet is a huge key to my success, and from there I send people to my transformation highway:

It starts with The Empowered Messenger/gifts page, where people arrive and have the opportunity to receive free gifts. I also offer a complimentary one-on-one SEE or Strategic Empowerment Evaluation appointment to work with me in a deeper way, and a complimentary subscription to our Multimedia Email Magazine "Dancing on The Empowered Edge" and Resource Center for Messengers on the Path of Empowered Sacred Service.

My lower-ticket product is Feel Safe Speaking and a bigger-ticket product is Feel Safe and Powerful Asking for Money, priced at $1997 for the home study version. When I speak I package it with seven live mentorship open calls for $4997 and add a bonus ticket to the Empowered Messengers Business Builders Retreat.

The two-day Empowered Messenger Business Builders Retreat is valued at $4997. I give an Inspired Action Scholarship for on-the-spot buyers of 50% off, which comes to $2497. This is an intimate, by-invitation-only two-day retreat limited to eight people where we focus deeply and intently on each person's business in a Laser "Love" Seat for 90 minutes, and everyone in the group supports each other. It's a mini-mastermind. I can also bundle it instead with Feel Safe and Powerful Asking for Money.

To work privately with me, I offer a half-day Empowered Messenger Healing or Empowered Messenger Business Design Retreat. At the highest end, I offer either a half or full-year private Empowered Messenger Master Mentorship, which ranges from $25,000 to 6-figures.

Of course all of this is subject to evolution, so if you have this book in your hands several years from now some of my programs and pricing may be different. We are always, as Lisa says often, building the plane as we fly it. The important point to understand is that Lisa's teachings provide a FRAMEWORK and structure that allows you to be super creative AND make the connection with your client base that will serve them in the highest way possible.

Most access roads to work with me are offered via speaking. That's where my Speak-to-Sell-talk is vital! My bio, speaker packet, talk title, questions for the host and headshots were done right away—all the things Lisa teaches us to get ready. In addition I put into place all of the backend auto responders, teleseminar phone lines and sales pages that allow for promoters and virtual event organizers to host me to their communities with the greatest of ease on their end.

I made it known I wanted to be on radio shows, and telesummits. In the second Sassy year I was booked on over 100 speaking gigs, including radio shows and over 80 telesummits. A telesummit is a themed event where the host gathers a group of speakers. I did my own telesummit event at the end of 2010 called the 6-Figure Speakers Telesummit, where I invited Lisa to be the keynote speaker. I built credibility for myself as a host, built my list and got exposure on my speakers' lists. It was a wonderful way to bring my gift to a multitude of different audiences.

I've been on telesummits where there have been 50, even 75 speakers. Because I have everything set up on the backend, I'm ready to make offers. In the Sassy Mastermind, I am the Queen of Virtual Speaking, having spoken on 100+ virtual stages in one year.

I ended my first year with a $40,000 bottom line revenue, starting from $400. The second year I spoke at 25 different events between radio shows and telesummits and generated $174,000. The bulk of that was from speaking, inviting people to my gifts page and then inviting them into a one-on-one conversation to see if they were fit for my leveraged group program. Then in 2011, I was on

100 different stages and my business generated $190,000 in revenue.

In every opportunity I have to be of service, whether through products, programs or speeches, the transformation I offer is for messengers to prepare to be heard by millions, so they can spread their message of hope, harmony, wholeness and healing. And I'm proud to say Lisa has personally given me the opportunity to support her in that area as well.

Grab your free gift from Amethyst Wyldfyre at <u>www.MeetTheSassies.com</u> today.

Building Profits for Artful Success

by
Tonya Davidson

My mom and I owned two paint-it-yourself pottery studios for 10 years where I taught various art techniques while marketing this novel concept as new entertainment in Tucson. Teaching technique was rewarding but it didn't feel as if it was my sole purpose. People started asking where to get supplies for the techniques I taught them, so we decided to start a new business selling artist's materials. Borrowing $5000 from the studio business, we began selling art supplies all over the world out of my garage (sneaking workers in and out due to residential restrictions). Within three years Whole Lotta Whimsy was a 7-figure business!

For years I've been teaching classes all over the country for one of the largest international jewelry companies, and I was also meeting artists all over the world at trade shows where we'd sell our supplies. Most of them were struggling. In general, artists have no business background and find it difficult to market their work without feeling completely overwhelmed.

I realized I have a gift, helping artists understand business principles and teaching them how to market their businesses. I started helping customers for free while I was selling them tools and supplies, silver and gold (over 3,500 different items), giving them advice on how to take their businesses to the next level. Once I was exposed to the coaching world, I realized that was where my teaching gift came in and that's what I passionately wanted to do. I didn't want to sell tweezers anymore, I wanted to change lives exponentially by showing artists how to get out into the world so people could experience their blessings—their art.

Art is an extension of the artist, there is a special energy when art is created that is meaningful, and when art is purchased by someone who appreciates it, or given to someone with love, they get to feel that energy exchange. If I can help artists to touch people, I have also touched and blessed those people in some way as well.

The first thing I did was hire a coach, but I just couldn't get anywhere. Then I listened to Lisa's *Invisible Close*, and her Event Profit Secrets preview call in 2011. I have spoken at many artist conferences, but I was hesitant to offer to help them because artists are careful about how they spend their money. They work hard for it, and art is not as lucrative as it once was.

Attending Lisa's Event Profit Secrets three-day

event, I saw the possibility of helping people in a genuine way that isn't all about the money but about transformation. That made all the difference, and I signed up for both of Lisa's 6-Figure Teleseminar Secrets and Speak-to-Sell Bootcamps, as well as the Sassy Mastermind.

I knew my first onramp to my coaching business would be an online class because my customers live all over the world. Since my clients are visual, I turned that information into a webinar with slides to go along with the teleseminar. That worked out great and over 703 virtually attended. I never could have done it without the secrets and steps Lisa taught me. I already knew about teleseminars because I had been on several. But Lisa gave me the "how-to" so I could engineer my own webinar alone, in-house, without hiring anyone. I made an offer and 55 people signed up, earning me $29,800 my first time out.

My transformation highway has many levels. I still own the art supply company and I have a freebie on that website for a giveaway technique tutorial, plus a free e-zine that comes out twice a month. A lot of the people on that list are also on my Artful Success™ Coaching business list. On that website I have a Take Flight Four Pack. I give away two video tutorials on technique, one artistic alignment tool (a worksheet for artists to align their goals for the year), and an e-zine.

The Four Pack has a visual, writing and reading component, so I'm able to engage people with the learning style that is most effective for them.

I show prospective clients that I am not only a coach but also an artist, and I connect with them on both levels. I send each e-zine twice a month, and since most of my contacts are on both lists, they get an e-zine every week. One week from one company the subject will be a technique or tool or about art and design, and the next week there will be topics such as marketing, personal growth, overcoming overwhelm and other helpful business tips.

I assist artists with any kind of sales, from selling on a stage to wording a basic e-mail so it doesn't sound salesy. When I speak at a 20th annual artist conference this summer, I will finally make an irresistible offer from the stage, using the same Speak-to-Sell concept I use whether I'm writing a newsletter or a speech: Lisa's problem/solution, problem/solution method. I implement that in everything I do.

The other way I invite people onto my highway is being very active in social media, on Facebook, Pinterest and Twitter. I post items of value that my customers want to know. I'll highlight promotions for a teleclass that link back my website and e-zine so they can sign up for the call.

Artful Coaching's highest-ticket offering is my

Profitable Artist Development Program, starting with a 12-week mastermind program. Level One is called Foundations For Artful Success and it's about clarity, creating your voice, developing a niche, getting organized, increasing productivity and help with mindset for pricing and selling points. I teach that it's not the material that allows artists to charge $1300 for a ring instead of $85— it's the mindset and the compelling story about the item!

Level Two is called Building Profits For Artful Success, which covers marketing, social media, how to be accepted into galleries, establishing your own website, branding and Internet exposure.

When I help artists with branding, I tell them their own name is important, not their business name, because people remember artists by their names. And if something isn't selling, I help them tweak their collection to create a story and a mystique around the item so their work can be sold in upscale avenues rather than along with two million other jewelry listings on Etsy (a popular website offering handmade items for sale).

I am a how-to person and I have great ideas that I share with my students, the way Lisa does it: Here's step one, step two, here are examples to follow . . . No one does it that way but Lisa. Many coaches teach theory but none of them teach the actual nuts and bolts or the step-by-step methods. I've experienced coaches who come from a place of lack where they think if they give it all away you won't need them anymore. I think it's actually the opposite with Lisa because there are people who have been in her program for three years and they're still signing up and renewing their mastermind membership. You don't see that in other programs. Her group has more people who can implement than any group I've ever seen. I do what she does, allowing my clients to benefit from my experience, knowing the more I give, the more business I will have and the more artists I can help.

Grab your free gift from Tanya Davidson
at <u>www.MeetTheSassies.com</u> today.

Step Four
Live on
Planet *Sassy*

> "And the day came when the risk to remain tight in a bud was more painful than the risk it took to blossom."
>
> **—Anais Nin**

Chapter Ten
Defy Gravity

Navigating the Himalayas

As I mentioned in the beginning of the book, being an entrepreneur is a wonderful ride that can give you the highest highs of your life with some valleys in between. If you prefer the flatlands, it's perfectly fine to keep a job and stay an employee. But when you're supposed to be in the Himalayas and you're living in the flatlands, life can be painful.

I remember my big moment, sitting in the audience deciding whether to invest in the $100,000 mastermind. There I was turning 40, and my then-husband was in the last year of his cardiothoracic surgery fellowship. After ten long years, he would finally be a heart surgeon—he'd be making money. Life was about to get very comfortable for me. Deep inside I knew if I didn't make that leap now, I'd miss my window. It felt like my last chance to use my hunger and fire to find out what I could achieve in my life.

Following the taps and taking imperfect, inspired action is not always easy, but how easy is it to live a life of compromise, knowing you haven't lived up to your potential? Here are some tools to help you navigate the Himalayas.

Embrace the Trapeze

As you all know by now, God can't course-correct you when you're standing still. You've got to move, and imperfect action is the way to move. But what has really become apparent to me is that even greater than imperfect action is taking inspired action.

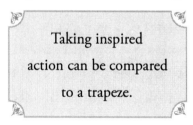

Taking inspired action can be compared to a trapeze.

Inspired action is where you have a little thought and you want to dismiss it because it's too crazy, or it's inconvenient, or it's totally not in line with the plans that you were making. The only way I can describe it is that you see this great opportunity that wasn't in your plans, and you know it was inspired because you didn't really think of it yourself.

Taking inspired action can be compared to a trapeze. Many of you are on this trapeze right now—

you're holding on and you're swinging on your trapeze. And then an inspired thought comes and suddenly that other trapeze appears faintly in the distance. Sometimes you can't even see it, you just sense that it's there. As you have this inspired thought, you imagine this other trapeze swinging toward you. What has to happen for you to get from this trapeze to that other trapeze, from where you are to what you see is possible? You have to let go.

Worse than that, you have to fly through the air untethered for a little while. It could be a nanosecond. There you are flying through the air, not holding onto anything, with no safety net.

The problem is we get onto this trapeze, as I did when I was with the understanding men company, and we want to hold on forever. I was swinging, it felt so good, I knew my purpose, I was out of that ache and that pain of not knowing what I was doing with my life, and then came the time to let go. That time of flying through the air before I caught the new trapeze was unsure, painful, scary and uncomfortable – terrifying actually. I had nothing to hold onto except a bit of faith when I could access it. But it was also a great way to grow.

Are you between the trapezes right now?

When it happens, acknowledge that you've let go, because you wouldn't be between the trapezes if you didn't. Just know that you are in the space between, and the minute that next bar crystallizes in front of you, it is going to be your job to reach out and grab it.

> Embrace those in-between moments. As uncomfortable as they are, they can change the course of your life and they only come along once in a while.

A few years ago I did a joint venture with a well-known internet marketer. We designed and sold a very successful training together. I'd seen something in her e-newsletter a few months before we came together and because I got inspired by it, I shot out of bed at 4:00 am and e-mailed her about working together.

It was just an inspired thought and I put it out there.

There were many times I'd written her and never gotten a response. I fully expected not to get one this time, but this was different—here I was, shot out of bed in the middle of the night. It had to be for a reason.

So I went on with my morning and 45 minutes later she responded, "Wow, Lisa, I was looking for something to do in October. This is perfect." It was August. Our training was launched within 60 days.

This training put me on the map at a whole new level and gave my career a huge boost. And it came from inspired action.

So one of the things that can't really be taught but can be suggested is to take inspired action, listen to your intuition and the little whispers and taps, and then go for it. Really, the worst that could have happened when I sent that email was that she wouldn't respond to me. But she did, and it brought me into a whole new world of access and influence, and served many people in the process.

Recognize Resistance (Internal)

Once you begin to take the leap, letting go and reaching for that new trapeze (the new inspired vision you have for yourself) you can count on the fact that you'll encounter some resistance. When you take quantum leaps in any area it's going to rock other people's boats—sometimes more than your own. Certainly, you'll have to deal with the reaction of spouses, friends and onlookers. However, in most cases the largest resistance you'll run into is from inside yourself.

I'll never forget when I registered for the $100,000 mastermind, with two toddlers at home and my then-hubby still in med school. My wonderfully supportive CPA (who regularly delights in how well things have turned out) worried about my sanity as I withdrew every penny I had from all of our savings and retirement accounts and began taking out credit. While it was tough to move forward in the face of other people's loving cautions, the tougher job was dealing with myself—my own fears, my own concerns, and my own insecurities, which all rose to the surface as I took this huge step.

But I did have encouragement. As Steven Pressfield says in the awesome book, *The War Of Art,* "If Resistance couldn't be beaten, there would be no Fifth Symphony, no *Romeo and Juliet,* no Golden Gate Bridge. Defeating Resistance is like giving birth. It seems absolutely impossible until you remember that women have been pulling it off successfully, with support and without, for fifty million years."[7]

In the same book, Pressfield comments that:

"The professional, although he accepts money, does his work out of love. He has to love it. Otherwise he wouldn't devote his life to it of his own free will ... The more you love your art/ calling / enterprise, the more important its accomplishment is to the evolution of your soul, the more you will fear it and the more Resistance you will experience facing it. The payoff of playing-the-game-for-money is not the money ... The payoff is that playing the game for money produces the proper professional attitude

---

7   Steven Pressfield, *The War of Art* (New York: Black Irish Entertainment LLC, 2012).

... Technically the professional takes money. Technically, the pro plays for pay. But in the end, he does it for love."

The way I see this in my own life is that rather than seeing resistance as a signal to stop, I use it as an indicator that I'm on the right track with something really important. And, as *The War of Art* points out, when you do sit down to do your art, there are angels and muses who come to your aid. As Pressfield further spells out:

"Like a magnetized needle floating on the surface of oil, Resistance will unfailingly point to true North - meaning that calling or action it most wants to stop us from doing ... We can use this. We can use this as a compass, we can navigate by Resistance, letting it guide us to that calling or action that we must follow before all others ... Rule of thumb: The more important a call or action is to our soul's evolution, the more Resistance we will feel toward pursuing it."[8]

Said another way:

"The enemy is a very good teacher."

– The Dalai Lama.

---

8   *The War of Art.*

Expect the Illusion (External)

One of the other things you can count on is that you will be visited by what one of my early spiritual teachers called The Illusion. What is The Illusion? It's that force that shows up to convince you that you can't do it. It's that external event that shakes you and weakens your confidence. I remember a lady I knew who decided to make an investment in a program with someone we both trusted. She was losing faith, and she said to me, "I don't know if I should do it because my credit card isn't processing and I think that's a sign."

I said, "No, that's The Illusion. You made a big commitment—you're stepping up, you're breaking through something—and The Illusion is right there to keep you small. Once you move forward beyond The Illusion, everything will shift for you."

You can count on The Illusion testing you, and I want you to do your best to recognize it. You've got to be able to tell yourself, "Okay, I'm in The Illusion. Pretty cool that it's there, that means I'm stepping up. That means I'm flying between the trapezes. That means something big is about to happen." You might as well just plan for it, even be on the lookout for it, that way it won't throw you off when it happens. It will be your sign that you're playing big.

What do I need to do NEXT? The "Get out of Overwhelm FAST question"

Here you are, look at you—you're on the road Living Sassy! You're getting your Unique Branded System together, trusting your inspired "taps" by taking imperfect action, making your irresistible offers, and learning how to leverage your systems to serve your clients at a deeper level. You've got a lot to do and it's easy to feel overwhelmed.

Here's my simple solution when you start to feel like it's all too much. Ask yourself: "What do I need to do next?" If you've got a list of 50 items to check off, of course you'd be overwhelmed, and overwhelm can leave you frozen, which doesn't serve you. But if you can identify the one thing you need to do next, that *does* serve you because after you do that one thing, you'll be standing in a new place and you will feel like a different, more confident person having that one accomplishment under your belt.

Then look at your list again and say, "What do I need to do next?" And what you decide to do next is going to be different than if you tried to put everything in order from the onset. Suddenly you'll have new parts of yourself available that weren't available before you got that first thing done. I learned this from an early mentor of mine, Alison Armstrong, and it has served me well in being the most inspired, empowered version of myself.

Learn the true story behind how this book came to be. Yes, it was all about taking Inspired Action. I made a private video about it and would love to share it with you to inspire your next big action. You can access it at <u>www.Sassy21DayChallenge.com</u>.

How Putting Myself First Paid Me and My Son

by
Sue Paananen

O ne of the problems people have starting their own business is letting go of their day job. It's a scary thing, but it can prevent you from really growing your business. Some people let go of it too soon and their business crashes with no funds. When should you let go of the trapeze? You don't want to let go of it as a rookie trapeze artist and hurt yourself so badly when you fall that you can't get back up again. You want to be practiced with your business, how you market it, how you do sales, and how you get clients. You want to build up your skills and be graceful with the transition.

I was working as a Senior Software Engineer when I was laid off in 2009. After deciding to start my own business, the company offered me my job back. My friends and family said, "Take the job, everyone's getting laid off!" So I did, but continued pursuing my own business as an Internet marketer. I was able to pay my bills with my day job and use some savings for extra training and coaching for my new business.

A year after starting my business, I joined the Sassy

Mastermind. I *really* wanted to resign from the day job I still had in order to focus full-time on my business, but my business mentors told me to wait until I had five to six months of consistent income from my business.

Three factors that finally made me feel ready to let go of my day job were clarity, clients, and pricing. I needed to have a clear vision of what I was doing and the ability to articulate that to others, a client base ready to hire me after dropping my day job, and the confidence to price my services appropriately. The Sassy Mastermind group helped me greatly in all of these areas.

I was horrible with pricing, charging people next to nothing. I came from humble beginnings and I was not accustomed to charging prices that were high in my mind. Lisa Sasevich gave me a golden piece of advice when I went to her house for a day of masterminding that helped me successfully let go of my day job four months later.

Lisa asked me how much I made per hour at my day job and what I would need to earn to replace that. Looking at it that way, I realized I wouldn't need to charge enormous prices or have very many clients to replace my income from my job. I instantly started getting clients. Each month my business doubled as I received passionate referrals. I gradually raised my prices and offered bundled packages, and last month I was less than $500 short of making 5 figures in one month.

Lisa was able to focus on my own individual story and give advice that fit my situation.

My business is called EEK! I Need a Geek! This name came from feedback from the Sassy group and proved to be a very "juicy" business name that grabbed everybody's attention, made everyone smile or laugh, related to their pain and need, and didn't need explaining.

I am an Online Presence Strategist and I work with women entrepreneurs who want to get their message out into the world, but don't want to worry about the technical headaches of implementation. In addition to helping with websites, I help my clients build their online foundation of gifts pages, preview call invite pages, strategy session applications, and follow up e-mail sequences. Then I help them build their list of people and expand their online reach through course launches, e-zine strategies, blogging strategies, article writing, and press releases.

Joining the Sassy Mastermind inspired me to change my focus from the Internet marketing business I began to serving these amazing individuals and other women like them by getting their missions out into to the world. I love how I can uniquely serve them, knowing the language and strategies of planet Sassy, setting me apart from others with Internet marketing and technical skills.

The Sassy Mastermind is the best community I have ever been in, full of heart-based entrepreneurs who are passionate in their businesses. They're helping people overcome cancer, helping veterans develop the life they want, helping their clients become financially stable, and so much more. I love working with people who have burning missions and am honored to be their strategist and tech support person when they need help to get their message out and to implement the strategies we learn.

About six months into my first year as a Sassy, I had to navigate around some very rough terrain in my business path, that made me want to hang onto my trapeze and never let go, and even crawl back up on it and walk back down the stairs in retreat. It was tax time, and in rounding up my expenses, I saw that there was a huge disparity between what I had spent for all my training and coaching compared to my income from my business. At the same time, my son and I were filling out college entrance forms and I was faced with a choice: college for my son or another year as a Sassy for me. I couldn't do both.

For about three weeks during the college enrollment period I became very depressed trying to decide if I should continue with my business or quit it and only stay with my day job to send my son to college. It tore at my heart because the desire to do my passion business was competing against my desire to be a good mother and let my son go to college. I had some heartfelt talks with my son, and he encouraged me to continue with my business. He had been one of my biggest cheerleaders as I was building my business. So with many hugs to him, I made the hard decision that my son could work for what he wanted just as I was doing—he'd be more inner-directed and motivated, and really appreciate college knowing the hard work that it took him to get there. So he worked, and my business took off, doubling every month from then on. By the 10th month, I was able to quit my job and sign up for my second year in the Sassy Mastermind.

Just three months into my second Sassy year, I made as much as I did at my day job and I'd earned back my investment with Sassy. Just one month later, my income doubled what I made in my day job. I am *so* glad I rejoined the Sassy Mastermind to have continued support as I further leverage my business. I timed my scary letting go of the trapeze well, and I was now defying gravity.

Not only that, but my son was able to start college in the winter semester instead of in the fall, which was a huge victory! I was so proud of him, and he was so appreciative, knowing we both had worked so hard for it. He was able to go to his first choice college in Boston, and I'd wanted to visit Boston for 20 years to see its amazing history, but never had the chance to do so. It was a huge milestone for both of us to go there when our dreams became an accomplished reality for us.

Being in the Sassy Mastermind group has been an incredible journey for me, from navigating the Himalayas to defying gravity to dancing in the spotlight with all of the others. Everybody there is so authentic, so motivated, and so much fun! It's the best family ever, and we all help each other so much! The second year is even sweeter than the first. It's like I'm in college myself – first as a freshman, then as a sophomore. I wanted to be a role model to my kids in continuing with my business; I hadn't worked on something for this long only to end up quitting. I was able to show my children they too could put their hearts into their own goals and accomplish their dreams.

Grab your free gift from Sue Paananen
at www.MeetTheSassies.com today.

Letting Go of My Job to Catch My Big Dream

by

Rochéle Lawson

C an you imagine working 24 hours a day seven days a week? That's what I did for seven years until I defied gravity and let go of one trapeze to fully grab the other. I was running a successful communications company by day and working as a registered nurse on the night shift. I'd work until 5:00, 6:00, sometimes 8:00 at night, maybe catch an hour of sleep, shower and get ready for the next nursing shift.

My husband and I started All Day Cable, Inc. in 1990 and by 1993 we had two kids. When my son was in preschool, I would put the baby down for a nap and catch two hours. By then we had office staff, so I migrated into sales and business operations, keeping contracts and proposals flowing behind the scenes.

But my heart and soul's passion was being a nurse: I truly, truly loved working in the ER. I excelled at it, it was my thing. I was the only female RN on an all-male shift and that was fabulous, we had a great team and worked well together. I took care of life flight nursing and the most challenging cases.

However, we could be very short staffed, and patient safety became an issue. There were times when attending physicians wouldn't admit a sick patient, and they'd be back days later, terribly ill. Those doctors got to know if it was my patient, you'd better just admit him.

One night it was just too much, we were short-staffed and I was crazy busy, with four patients all having heart attacks. It was during this night that I decided since my ability to give my patients the best care possible was being hampered by hospital bureaucracy, I needed to make a change for the better. Our telecommunication installation business was growing, my kids were growing too, so I told my husband I was quitting my nursing job, even though we were losing the security of a stable check coming in (and great benefits). Yet for my own sanity I needed to step away from the ER.

In all honesty, it was quite traumatic to leave it behind. I was good at it and I *knew* I was good at it. I was very intuitive; I could look at a person and tell how sick they were. The physicians would always tell me, "You should have stayed in school," or "You should go back to school and become a doctor." They would ask me what I thought was wrong with a patient and which labs or tests I would run.

Once I let go of the ER, more opportunities started

coming in for the telecommunication installation business and it grew astronomically. We set up network distribution systems for customers throughout the western states and acquired some very large customers, many still with us 21 years later. I sat on the board of the National Association of Women Owned Businesses for seven years and became president. During that time I received media exposure because I was a female minority business owner of a telecommunication installation company in a male-dominated industry.

When my husband and I went to a meeting, the major customers knew him, but they would think I was his secretary. He would say, "That's Rochéle, she's the owner and Chief Executive Officer." They would flip out because I looked 15. That always made us laugh.

Because my true purpose is health and wellness, I went back to school and obtained a Master's Degree in holistic health and wellness. In 2010, I opened The Health, Healing & Wellness Company. I did a speaking engagement just from what I learned listening to Lisa's products after seeing her speak at an eWomenNetwork event in 2011 and made 5-figures in a 75-minute talk. I didn't really have a structure and what I offered wasn't totally put together, but as Lisa says, it just needs to be "good enough." If I could do that from listening to free talks, what would happen if I became a Sassy? I joined the Sassy Mastermind to grow my new business, another let-go-and-live-your-dream trapeze stunt.

My dream has always been to have a holistic wellness center with on-site cabanas in a pristine and beautiful setting, like the Miraval Spa where Lisa occasionally holds Sassy retreats. My true passion is to bring health and wellness to the lives of individuals who don't know what is possible, or don't know where to find help. I am an Ayurvedic Health Practitioner. I used herbal remedies even as a child, made my own herbal facials as a teen, and never had acne. I've been getting regular massages since I was 18. I'm also a Certified Meditation Specialist.

Becoming a Sassy has been tremendous. I wish I'd known Lisa 21 years ago when I started the telecom business because we could have conquered the world! Being a Sassy has enlightened me with a wealth of opportunities and information to structure my new business for success.

Everything I do is based on a person's unique body type. If someone wants help with stress, dietary issues, weight management, high blood pressure, cholesterol or any other health problem, I take a full "before" assessment, come up with a 90-day plan to eliminate toxins and bring them back into balance, which may require the utilization of herbs, spa therapies and meditation, just to name a few. From there, I have six-month and 12-month programs, and offer Blissful Living Retreats at fabulous resorts with two days of spa therapies, yoga, meditation and healthy eating.

No two people will ever have the exact same health plan, that's what is so special, unique and beautiful about this business. It's not cookie-cutter like allopathic Western medicine—which I'm very familiar with! Two people with high blood pressure will not receive the same treatment because the root of the issue is different for each of them.

I'm not new to the business arena. I've spoken on Capital Hill for Women Owned Businesses, but I've never experienced anything like the Sassy community in my life. It's phenomenal. It's not just Lisa. The Sassy camaraderie helps you because you don't even know how successful you can be. The other Sassies see it in you, but you don't see it because it's right at the tip of your nose. I love it—words can't describe how much. I've never had this; it's always been me, alone. To have a group of people like this warms my heart every time I think about them or talk about them.

I've been a Sassy for five months, and my business has increased 40%. Clients are able to find me. I have a radio show and I'm getting more visibility. I'm guest writing for other people's blogs and doing radio spots on other people's radio shows or teleseminars. I'm actually living the Sassy Life!

My book was released at the beginning of 2012, *Intro to Holistic Health Ayurvedic Style*, and I don't think that would have happened if I didn't have my ducks in a row from what I learned with the Sassy Mastermind; I wouldn't have been ready.

Now I'm letting go of the telecommunications installation company completely. I've been through it before, and I know that once I let go, my wings will fully expand, open, and I will soar. I know I will reach the highest heights that I have ever imagined.

Grab your free gift from Rochéle Lawson at www.MeetTheSassies.com today.

Living Proof that ANYTHING is Possible

by

Dr. Venus Opal Reese

My work is about "Who are you—for yourself?" Most people can't answer that question. They can talk about roles—mom, dad, entrepreneur—but alone at night in the dark, all they see is what they're not. I work with high achievers who get their meaning, their sense of self, from outside themselves. When people are highly successful, it doesn't necessarily mean that they are fulfilled.

I spend most of my time listening to what people aren't saying, and supporting and empowering them to create a relationship with themselves; not one that's inherited, not one that's derived from outside stimuli, but from inner peace and joy. Then my clients start learning, loving, and living their worth in record time.

If you are not moved to tears by who you are and always have been, you don't know your worth. And if you don't know, you are stepping over money, you are stepping over success, because what got you *here* won't get you *there—wherever "there" is for you in terms of success and fulfillment.* Conversely, all the tricks that you used that made you successful are the same ones that undermine effectiveness in your interpersonal relationships – including your relationship with yourself.

For example, what makes you an independent, strong woman could also get you divorced. I tell people, "It's okay to be independent, but it's okay to receive too. You don't have to be right all the time. Let someone love you once in a while."

I don't think of myself as a "success." My life has been about just trying to survive. The only thing that I am certain of is that God loves me and that my life was spared for something greater. I have a sister who died after doing heroin laced with embalming fluid, I have a brother who was in and out of jail for selling drugs, and I have a younger sister who had her first kid when she was 16. By the time I was 16, I was living on the streets.

I grew up in Baltimore, right around the corner from Johns Hopkins University. One day I was sitting on the corner literally steeped in piss and beer thinking to myself, "How did I get here, how do I get out? God please help me." It was a very simple prayer. The answer to my prayer came in the form of a teacher— my Ninth Grade Math teacher, Mrs. Judy Francis. I came to school the next day and my odor preceded me. I was unkempt and I didn't have the means to care for myself. Kids teased me while teachers walked away pretending they didn't notice—except for Mrs. Francis. She helped me get cleaned up and gave me a warm meal. She dropped me back off at my street corner, and she never asked me to explain.

Where I come from, that's a big deal. I didn't have to lie, and I was able to keep my dignity. It was her willingness to not shame me along with not having to articulate what put me on the street that gave me the desire to spend time with her, because I knew I wouldn't have to talk. I would hang out after school to wipe down her board and I'd wait long enough until she took me for food and then dropped me back at my corner.

This went on for a very long while and we developed a trust relationship in the unsaid. (Where I come from you never tell. Snitching is death for real. You do *not* talk.)

I started to read books in her math class because she would let me. Finally after about six months, Mrs. Francis marched to the back the classroom and said, "Look, if you're not going to talk, then write." She shoved a pencil and pad into my hand. She had been giving me food, so I felt obligated, and my thoughts came out as poetry. Mrs. Francis read them, typed them up and sent them off to an NAACP competition. I won.

When I realized what Mrs. Francis had done for me, the closest analogy I could think of was Helen Keller and her teacher Annie Sullivan. In *The Miracle Worker,* the moment Helen connected W-A-T-E-R with that invisible force running over her hand, she became a sentient being. She was pulled out of the darkness of blindness and deafness and muteness and attained consciousness. When I comprehended what Mrs. Francis had done for me, I too became a sentient being. It was the first time in my life I was separated from the pain I understood as my life. My pain was not me.

It gave me a new thought: the way Mrs. Francis sees me is different from how I see me. I saw me as worthless, literally with no intrinsic value at all, with evidence to prove it for generations. But Mrs. Francis saw me as somebody who matters. And I thought, if I matter, **maybe** I *can* do something with my life. My actions started to be those of somebody who mattered, somebody who had worth. The next thing was: maybe I can get an education.

Today, I have four degrees including a 2nd Masters degree and Ph.D. from Stanford University, I did a successful show off-Broadway, and started my own business.

The truth is you can never outperform your self-image. Your net worth will never exceed your self-worth.

I want my life to be living proof that anything is possible. But at first when I got out there to speak, audiences would clap and shed tears, but not buy anything. Lisa and the Sassy Mastermind allowed me to systematize my story so it could reach the masses. When I found Lisa's methods, I started to weep. Her words and approach were so humane, gentle and clear. The first time I used her Speak-to-Sell model I cleared $15,000 in 45 minutes, and then I did it again and made another $15,000 from the stage. I used Lisa's ACTION Sales Secrets to close a $10,000 CEO client. My tele-seminar led to my first workshop, "Leveraging Your Worth for Outrageous Wealth" where I made $26,000 with my very own "Self-Worth and Wealth" Diamond Customized Mentorship.

Lisa teaches us Sassies to Defy Gravity, to defy who you think you are and listen to your heart. What I do is Defy the Impossible. I am able to hear other people's hearts, and allow them to face themselves. I give my students tools to love, live and leverage their worth in the world. When they come to me, they are living with their inherited selves, how family sees them, what society says they "should" do or be, and with their reactionary self that came when life broke their hearts and they said, "Never again."

My story is about Defying the Odds. Mrs. Francis allowed me dignity in my silence, and listened to what

I wasn't saying. Now I listen to the silence so I can teach humanity how to discover their own worth, celebrate it, and give it center stage.

Grab your free gift from Dr. Venus Opal Reese at <u>www.MeetTheSassies.com</u> today.

Get Started Living *Sassy* Today

W

e're here to support you in creating your Sassy Life so you too can make big money and a big difference doing what you love. Join us TODAY for our free 21-Day Live Sassy Challenge at www.Sassy21DayChallenge.com

This is your complimentary three-week pass to Life on Planet Sassy. You'll be receiving Lisa's Sassy Guidance daily in your email inbox to walk you step-by-step toward creating the life of your dreams.

This is also the place to access all of the immediately useful bonus video trainings, worksheets and action guides mentioned throughout this book.

Meet the Sassies

L isa and the Sassies have joined together to provide you with thousands of dollars of personal development and business resources to support you on your Sassy path.

Join us at www.MeetTheSassies.com to read inspiring stories of Sassy entrepreneurs just like you who are making big money and a big difference doing what they love—and collect your bonus Sassy resources today.

Sassy Resources

Join our Sassy community and connect with other heart-centered messengers and like-minded experts who are making a big difference and big money doing what they love!

 Facebook Fan Page <u>LisaSasevichfan.com</u>

Twitter @LisaSasevich

YouTube <u>YouTube.com/lisasasevich</u>

Linked In <u>LinkedIn.com/in/LisaSasevich</u>

We also suggest you visit <u>www.LisaSasevich.com</u> and sign up to receive my bi-weekly Invisible Close Sales Nugget e-newsletter and my FREE 6-part series, "Simple, Quick and Easy Ways to Boost Sales Without Spending a Dime."

This is the best way to keep updated on all things Sassy and receive ongoing Invisible Close advice from me on how to boost sales on stages, teleseminars, webinars and one-to-one without being salesy. You'll also receive invitations to complimentary trainings and upcoming courses and events we have scheduled.

Here are a few of our most popular home-study programs and live events to date:

The Invisible Close™
Turn Interested Prospects Into Invested Clients On-The-Spot Without Being Pushy or Salesy!

If you love what you do, but hate the sales part, The Invisible Close will teach you how to boost sales using Irresistible Offers and inspire your prospective clients to say YES to themselves on-the-spot. You can instantly make thousands of additional dollars each and every month without working any harder! Learn how Lisa Sasevich converts 100% of exactly the right people into happy, paying clients on-the-spot ... and how you can too.

The Invisible Close
6 Figure Teleseminar Secrets

Use My Clear, PROVEN 5-Step Plan to Make Money with Your Expertise!

Whether you're an expert who's just getting started or an experienced marketer, I'll show you exactly how to create those 6-figure launches again and again. Just follow this paint-by-numbers system to see great results in YOUR business.

You'll learn...

- How to CRAFT YOUR OFFER so that it's TRULY Irresistible.
- My STEP-BY-STEP formula to crafting YOUR PREVIEW CALL for BIG pay-day results.
- How to Fill your call with qualified prospects, hungry for what you have to offer.
- The most heavily guarded secrets on EXACTLY how the big guns TRIPLE sales after each pre-view call.
- Proven strategies for keeping the sales you've made and (more important), for turning them into HIGH-TICKET, BACK-END UPSELLS!
- All without being "salesy."

Speak-to-Sell Bootcamp

**Step into the Spotlight with a Talk that you Love,
Offers that Sell and the Confidence
that comes with being Ready**

- Massively increase your back-of-the-room sales
- Add speaking to your marketing mix
- Create a line of excited customers at your back table ready to purchase

The Speak-to-Sell Bootcamp is designed specifically for entrepreneurs, coaches, experts, speakers, authors and service professionals who prefer an authentic style of speaking and want to use their authentic style to draw people in without being "salesy."

About the Author

Lisa Sasevich, known by many as "The Queen of Sales Conversion," is the creator of the widely recognized "Invisible Close" sales conversion system and mother of the world-renowned "Sales, Authenticity and Success Mastermind"... aka "The Sassies!"

Her passion is to help experts who are making a difference get their message out and make big money doing what they love. In doing that, Lisa's own business quickly soared from $130,000 per year as a one-on-one mentor to over $2 million a year just 10 months later. She figured out what she was doing right, kept doing it, and doubled that again to over $4 million the year after that. Many call Lisa's meteoric success an entrepreneurial Cinderella Story, and the best part is, she's spent the last three years helping other messengers experience the same beautiful results.

Lisa started her career in the corporate world at Fortune 500 companies such as Hewlett-Packard and Pfizer Pharmaceuticals, consistently winning top sales awards, but always preoccupied by her true love of personal and spiritual development. Eventually she made the leap, followed her heart and went to work for a small seminar company that taught women to understand and create partnerships with men. In just three short years, Lisa's sales and marketing techniques contributed to growing that company from $300,000 to over $1 million—all with no marketing budget. This was also where she honed her skills of designing and presenting irresistible offers to inspire women to say "yes" to themselves on the spot. These skills eventually became the basis for what is now known as *The Invisible Close*.

Lisa was able to systematize her processes so other passionate heart-centered entrepreneurs and agents of change could be of service, market their own businesses and become known by getting out there with irresistible offers. Her formulas help small businesses attract more clients easily, without being pushy or salesy.

Lisa's methods are so successful they've been adopted by countless best-selling authors and thought leaders, many of whom have been in the business for more than 30 years. Now the mentors Lisa sought out early in her career are attending her workshops, signing up for private mentoring, and increasing their profits exponentially.

An enthusiastic, engaging and caring speaker, Lisa has made a difference in charitable circles, including winning the 2011 Foundation Champion Award for driving over $285,000 to eWomenNetwork's Foundation. Featured on stages all over the world, and recently in *WoW* and *Success* magazines, her reach is worldwide, with students from the United States, Canada, Europe, Australia, New Zealand and South America.

From her refreshing spiritual guidance and mind-expanding points of view, to her sales, speaking, marketing and leveraging acumen, Lisa helps gifted entrepreneurs, speakers, coaches, experts and consultants spend more time doing what they are meant to do—transforming lives in greater numbers.

CPSIA information can be obtained at www.ICGtesting.com
Printed in the USA
BVOW07s0812240913

331584BV00004B/10/P